d by
gel,
CFA

Life-Cycle Investing: Financial Education and Consumer Protection

RESEARCH FOUNDATION

OF CFA INSTITUTE

Statement of Purpose

The Research Foundation of CFA Institute is a not-for-profit organization established to promote the development and dissemination of relevant research for investment practitioners worldwide.

ISBN 978-1-934667-52-1

30 November 2012

Tribute

Our friend John Nagorniak, CFA, died on 7 September 2012 after a long illness. We at the Research Foundation of CFA Institute are saddened but will always be grateful for his remarkable accomplishments as a trustee from 2004 to 2011 and as our chair from 2008 to 2010. John's history bears testimony to his wide range of skills and his steady hand as chair. He possessed a rare combination of patience and calm through thick and thin. His ability to simplify complex issues and his keen devotion to pushing the frontiers of the Research Foundation's research will resonate forever.

He was a natural leader throughout his career, serving as:

- President and CEO of Franklin Portfolio Associates for more than 20 years

- Senior vice president and chief investment officer at State Street Bank and Trust Company

- Director of investment technology at John Hancock Mutual Life Insurance Company

- President of the Boston Security Analysts Society

- Director of the MIT investment committee

- Treasurer for his Princeton University class on several occasions

John was a graduate of Princeton University and the MIT Sloan School of Management. His array of capabilities, his generosity of time, and his spot-on insights made the businesses and organizations he touched significantly better. Perhaps his strongest contribution was to quantitative investment management in its formative stages. His deep understanding of the math behind groundbreaking discoveries was remarkable. But perhaps more remarkable was John's ability to convey the essence of those discoveries to others. He was a quintessential pioneer, interpreter, and practitioner.

The Research Foundation and CFA Institute community of more than 100,000 members worldwide express their heartfelt appreciation for John Nagorniak's lifetime devotion and their sorrow at losing such a friend. To his family, the Research Foundation expresses our deepest sympathies. We are grateful for the opportunity to have known and worked with such a gentleman.

Page 10 - Figure 3B = Mistake.
Corrected on handout.

Contents

CE Qualified Activity ✼ **CFA Institute** This publication qualifies for 5 CE credits under the guidelines of the CFA Institute Continuing Education Program.

Foreword

Financial education and consumer protection have, relatively recently and suddenly, come to be seen as vitally important tasks. Why now? Why not a century ago or a half century ago? More to the point, how did ordinary people, workers with no special talent for or interest in investing, get to be on their own in executing the daunting task of saving and investing for retirement and for other needs?

As Robert Merton points out in this book, we don't expect people to design and build their own cars. We do it for them, in a way that makes the technology so transparent that a 16-year-old can use it. The same goes for computers and all of the other important instruments of daily life. Why is saving and dissaving for retirement so "special" that it requires us to educate ourselves—and protect ourselves from fraud and misinformation—in a field for which most of us have no aptitude?

The answer lies in the changing way we live and in some legislative history from the middle of the last century. In traditional societies, the savings function is carried out within the family. Parents support their children, and then the children grow up and support their elders. In a more developed society, there may also be support from charities and government; Social Security began in the United States in 1935, following a model developed earlier in Germany. Back then, the burden on all these institutions was not very large because most people either did not retire or lived only a short time after retiring. People with extra resources could save them, as they do today, investing in bank deposits, bonds, equities, and insurance policies. Some skill in investment management developed that way, especially among the middle and upper classes.

By the 1940s, however, two factors combined to make employer-sponsored defined-benefit pension plans attractive to both the employer and the employee: (1) increasing longevity and (2) the transition of the United States from a low-income-tax society to a high-income-tax society. Increased longevity means a longer planning horizon with more risk, a situation best handled by institutions with substantial resources and investment talent: insurance companies, banks, and investment management firms. High taxes mean that deferring or avoiding taxation becomes very important, and unlike current compensation, deferred compensation (that is, a pension) is very lightly taxed under U.S. law. Employers responded by enriching pension promises instead of, or in addition to, current paychecks, in many cases obviating the individual's need to save and removing his or her incentive to develop investment skill.

The pension system worked well for a while, at least for the 40–50% of workers who were covered by well-managed plans. But when market returns turned sour in the 2000s, many employers—including governments, private companies, and to some extent, nonprofits—began to fall short on the promises. The bull markets of the 1980s and 1990s had produced the illusion, but not the reality, that fat investment returns would make up for skinny pension contributions; and as one pension after another was revealed to be radically underfunded, employers terminated the plans.

When looking back on the perceived "golden age" of defined-benefit pensions from the 1940s to the 1990s, we tend to overlook those who were not covered by the system or who were poorly covered. My grandfather is a case in point. He was a successful rabbi who was never short of money during his working lifetime. However, he faced two unforeseen risks. His rabbinical pension was not adjusted for the massive inflation that occurred in the late 1960s, 1970s, and early 1980s; and he lived to the age of 103. At the time of his death in 1991, he was receiving a pension in the microscopic amount of about $2000 per year (which would have been a survivable income a half century earlier). Fortunately, he was a self-educated investor and saved plenty of money, but despite that achievement, he ran out of money before he died. The golden age was not golden for everyone, and financial education has always been important.

When employers terminate defined-benefit plans, they usually put defined-contribution (DC) plans—which are savings plans, not pensions—in their place. DC plans have the advantage of being portable as workers change jobs, but that is just about their only advantage. Savings rates are whatever each participant wants them to be, which in most cases is far too low to support retirement under any investment return scenario. (The savings rate is also subject to strict upper limits that typically keep the contribution from being as large as it needs to be.) Individuals also turn out to be poor investors; they take too much risk (or occasionally not enough), buy high and sell low, and are insensitive to active management costs. DC-plan investing has mostly been a disaster, although a small minority of workers have retired rich on their DC plans, or will.

In addition, longevity risk has reached extreme levels and will only get "worse" (the scare quotes reflecting our view that longevity is to be highly prized, the only problem being how to pay for it). A professional career typically starts to pay off only in one's 30s or later and usually ends by 70—so that the income from 35 or 40 years of work needs to be stretched to pay for 70 or 75 years of life (figuring that the maximum possible life span is currently about 105 years). This model takes *a lot* of saving—there is only so much that investment skill can accomplish.

No wonder there is a pension-and-retirement crisis.[1] It is not insoluble. But it will take monumental effort. This book is an element of that effort.

Like the two previous volumes in this series, the current volume is based on the proceedings of an extraordinary conference organized by Professor Zvi Bodie of Boston University and sponsored by Boston University, the Federal Reserve Bank of Boston, and the Research Foundation of CFA Institute. This series of conferences differs from other gatherings in its interdisciplinary nature. Rather than bringing only finance academics and practitioners together, the conferences have included economists, lawyers, accountants, actuaries, regulators, corporate and union leaders, and media commentators. This diversity of speaker and author backgrounds gives the conferences and their associated books a unique flavor.

Professor Bodie has written an overview that contains a guide to the specific contents of this book, which we are exceptionally pleased to present. *Life-Cycle Investing: Financial Education and Consumer Protection* is invaluable reading for anyone concerned with the well-being of people in their roles as savers and investors.

Laurence B. Siegel
Gary P. Brinson Director of Research
Research Foundation of CFA Institute

REFERENCES

Waring, M. Barton. 2011. *Pension Finance.* Hoboken, NJ: John Wiley & Sons.

Novy-Marx, Robert, and Joshua Rauh. 2011. "Public Pension Promises: How Big Are They and What Are They Worth?" *Journal of Finance*, vol. 66, no. 4 (August): 1211–1249.

---

[1]For a description of the mess, see Waring (2011) and Novy-Marx and Rauh (2011).

Overview

Zvi Bodie
Norman and Adele Barron Professor of Management
Boston University

Many empirical studies have shown that U.S. households generally make significant financial mistakes. They spend at unsustainable levels and fail to save enough for old age, borrow more than they can afford to repay, pay interest rates that are higher than necessary, buy investment and insurance contracts with features they do not need—the list goes on. The 2008 financial crisis that emanated from subprime mortgage defaults starkly highlighted how such mistakes can not only harm the consumers who make them but also create an economic crisis that affects everyone, including many who made no mistakes.

Financial mistakes are made worse by three factors that might be controllable: ignorance, bad habits, and bad advice. Policymakers in government and the private sector who sincerely want to minimize the harmful effects of consumer financial mistakes need to understand how these three factors operate and interact in order to design and implement policies to control them. They require input from bona fide scholars in many scientific disciplines and from expert practitioners with scientific training.

In May 2011, we brought together academic researchers, educators, advisers, and regulators to discuss how household financial decisions might be improved through a combination of better education, better advice, and better oversight of business practices. The focus was on low- and middle-income (LMI) households. During two intense days at Boston University, we analyzed the gaps in consumers' current financial knowledge, how those gaps might be narrowed through financial education programs, and how consumer protection regarding financial products might be strengthened.[1]

The 2011 conference was the third in the Boston University series titled "The Future of Life-Cycle Saving and Investing," sponsored jointly by the Research Foundation of CFA Institute and the Federal Reserve Bank of Boston.[2]

---

[1]Selected videos from the 2011 conference are on the Boston University website (http://management.bu.edu/blog/2009/12/01/video-from-the-2011-future-of-lifecycle-saving-investing-conference/).

[2]Books from the 2006 and 2008 conferences are on the CFA Institute website (www.cfapubs.org). Note that the 2008 conference had seven sponsoring organizations: the Research Foundation of CFA Institute, the Federal Reserve Bank of Boston, the Employee Benefit Research Institute (EBRI), the Network for Studies on Pensions, Aging and Retirement (Netspar), the Professional Risk Managers' International Association (PRMIA), the Retirement Income Industry Association (RIIA), and the Society of Actuaries (SOA).

In the opening address, Nobel Laureate in Economic Sciences Robert C. Merton set the stage for subsequent discussions by posing five questions regarding financial education and consumer financial protection:

1. Are financial innovations and the tools from financial science and engineering essential to effectively address the consumer finance challenges of the future?

2. If "keep it simple" is, in fact, "keep it simple for the consumer," what does the phrase mean for regulators and service providers?

3. Is the behavioral dysfunction associated with choice in consumer finance "too many choices" or "too many nonmeaningful choices"?

4. Is intelligent product design and oversight an effective substitute for consumer financial education?

5. What should be the priority: educating financial consumers or educating fiduciaries?

Merton then addressed all of these questions in the context of employer-sponsored retirement plans. He framed his answer by first explaining the theory of optimal lifetime consumption, and then he explored how the theoretical optimum might be approximated in the real world by expert practitioners acting in the best interests of retirement plan participants. His answers can be summarized as follows:

1. The tools of financial science and engineering are essential to effectively address the challenges of retirement planning for consumers.

2. "Keep it simple for the consumer" will require greater complexity for service providers and regulators.

3. Consumers do not benefit from more choice unless the choices are meaningful to them.

4. Intelligent product design and oversight are more effective in improving consumer welfare than consumer financial education.

5. The priority for policymakers should be to educate fiduciaries.

In the six sessions that followed Merton's opening address, we discussed different aspects of the issues he raised. In each session, a panel composed of researchers, educators, and expert practitioners opened the discussion. We focused on the needs of LMI households and sought to identify best practices in the most consequential areas: housing, borrowing, saving, and investing. We included spending on career training in our discussion of saving and investing because such spending contributes to the accumulation of human capital. It is probably the single most consequential form of saving and investing.

In Session 1, we discussed best practices for financial educators and advisers. Educators help consumers gain the basic knowledge needed to make financial decisions, whereas financial advisers guide and assist them in making and implementing those decisions. Among the questions discussed were

- Just how bad are the financial decisions consumers make today?

- What is the potential gain from better decision making? From more suitable products?

- Who is getting professional advice? Is it good advice? If not, why not?

- What special efforts should be made to educate and guide LMI households?

Session 2 was about housing decisions. Purchasing and financing a home is perhaps the single most important financial decision households make. Among the questions addressed were

- What factors should a household take into account in deciding whether and when to buy a house and how to finance it?

- What can be done to improve the options available to households in choosing between buying or renting a house and the various financing alternatives?

Session 3 was centered on consumer credit, and it focused on the practices of the credit counseling industry. In recent years, the industry has been criticized for not operating in the best interests of consumers of credit. Some services have been accused of being collection agencies in disguise, and some have been convicted of consumer fraud. We discussed

- The typical mistakes made by low- and middle-income borrowers.

- The typical abusive practices of some lenders.

- How a consumer can distinguish between reputable credit counseling firms and firms that exploit their customers.

Session 4 addressed saving and investing by low- and middle-income households. The questions discussed were

- Do LMI households save too little?

- Do they have adequate incentives to save?

- How much risk should they take in their investment portfolios?

- Do means-tested government insurance programs, such as Medicaid, actually discourage saving and encourage excessive risk taking by LMI households?

Session 5 covered the lessons to be learned from past efforts to promote financial education. Many government agencies and nonprofit organizations have offered an array of resources intended to better equip consumers with essential financial knowledge.

- What type of campaigns have longer-lasting impact?

- What characteristics of the target audience are the most relevant, and how should these be taken into account in designing an effective financial literacy course?

- How can we best reach LMI households, which tend to be less financially savvy?

Session 6 looked at consumer financial protection. Although lax regulation may bear much responsibility for fomenting the subprime crisis, most observers would agree that consumer protection has not kept up with the rapid pace of innovations in consumer financial products. How should financial instruments marketed to consumers be regulated to minimize the potential for harm to buyers without stymieing innovation or creating incentives for regulatory arbitrage? In particular, should suitability rules be more stringent for financial products sold to LMI households?

In the pages that follow, you will read how the conference participants addressed all of these questions. There was general agreement that consumers of financial products and services make many costly mistakes. However, there was considerable disagreement about relying primarily on consumer financial education programs to correct those mistakes. So far, there is little evidence that the financial education programs in schools, libraries, community centers, and places of work have had any lasting effect in improving decision making by consumers.

Keynote Speaker: Merton

Observations on Financial Education and Consumer Financial Protection

Robert C. Merton
School of Management Distinguished Professor of Finance
Sloan School of Management
Massachusetts Institute of Technology

In developing the next generation of consumer financial and retirement plan services, we must develop truly effective ways to make consumers "smarter" about their retirement. In addition, however, we must ensure that the protections we put in place elicit, indeed encourage, the right behavior and do not thwart the ultimate goal of providing secure financial futures for consumers.

In my mind, five questions should be addressed regarding financial education and consumer financial protection:

1. Are financial innovations and the tools from financial science and engineering essential to effectively address the consumer finance challenges of the future?

2. If "keep it simple" is, in fact, "keep it simple for the consumer," what does the phrase mean for regulators and service providers?

3. Is the behavioral dysfunction associated with choice in consumer finance "too many choices" or "too many nonmeaningful choices"?

4. Is intelligent product design and oversight an effective substitute for consumer financial education?

5. What should be the priority: educating financial consumers or educating fiduciaries and other gatekeepers?

What follows is an attempt to examine these questions through the lens of a single consumer product of some significance. The product, which is one I've been working on, is a retirement solution for employer-provided plans.

Design Requirements for a Next-Generation Employer-Provided Pension Solution

The first thing to do when designing a new retirement solution for employer plans is to establish the goal. I propose that, in retirement, people want an income for life that will allow them a standard of living of the kind they enjoyed in the latter part of their work lives. The key is that the outcome needs to be a *standard of living*, which is best expressed as a financial goal by a stream of income for life, protected against inflation. Both Social Security benefits and defined-benefit pensions are expressed in terms of an income flow per year and not as an amount of wealth. Those familiar with Jane Austen know that in 18th century England, an important characteristic of a man in terms of his attractiveness to women was the standard of living he could provide. When Mr. Darcy—who is a catch in Austen's *Pride and Prejudice*—is described, he is not referred to as "worth £200,000." Rather, he's "worth £10,000 a year." A standard of living is a flow of income, not a single amount of money; the accumulation of wealth is simply a means to the goal of annual income adequate to support a designated standard of living. Wealth is not sufficient information to determine a sustainable standard of living. For example, $1 million at 4% supports a lifestyle of $40,000 a year, but in the current environment of a 0.60% real interest rate, it only supports a lifestyle of $6,000 a year!

Once the goal is established, the plan should satisfy other essential design characteristics. For example, it should be integrated—incorporating all current and future sources of retirement income. Additionally, if we accept the goal of income (rather than portfolio value), the measurement and management of the risk–return trade-off should be in terms of retirement income that is hedged for inflation, longevity, real interest rates, and of course, market risk.

Furthermore, and this aspect is important, the plan must be robust enough to work effectively without the luxury of a financial planner or even the inclination to participate in the plan. It is well-documented behavior that people tend not to engage in the investment process in their plan and, indeed, won't answer the questions needed for good decisions to be made for them. It was this common behavior of no engagement that motivated the adoption of "opt-out" versus traditional "opt-in" rules for joining a defined-contribution pension plan as part of the Pension Protection Act of 2006. In such plans, we cannot educate consumers directly because they're not even interacting with us!

This issue brings me to the next point: A common mantra is "Get the consumer engaged" when it comes to defined-contribution pensions. I would qualify that with "provided engagement improves the chances of achieving the goal." Participants who are induced to open a brokerage account in their IRA accounts may become quite engaged, trading stocks around the world on their computer after work, but it is almost a sure thing that this type of engagement will not improve, but actually diminish, the likelihood of success in reaching their goals. The best way to engage participants is with meaningful feedback and choice. You let them know candidly and clearly how they're doing. It's very much like a report from a medical checkup. I'm always hoping my doctor will say to me, "Oh! You're not only in great shape, but if I didn't know better, I'd think you were 10 years younger!" But if that statement isn't true, I want her to tell me. Otherwise, what's the point of getting a checkup? If she tells me I have a bad cholesterol level of 300—clearly not good—she also lets me know there's something I can do about it: Take statins, change my diet, exercise. Even if I don't want to hear her report of bad news that I have a serious problem, an honest assessment along with the steps that can be taken to fix it give me a way to address the problem.

In this framework, meaningful feedback and choices are given to people—the statins, the exercise, the diet—so that they can do something about the problem. What can people do to increase the likelihood of achieving the target retirement goal, their desired standard of living? You give them an easy way to implement those decisions—ideally, a way to "learn by doing," which in terms of providing education works infinitely better than a handbook or sending people to school.

In regard to consumer protection, the idea of giving participants prospectuses or even educational materials is not effective. What makes more sense is to direct resources to the fiduciaries—the plan sponsor and the sponsor's consultant—to ensure that *they* are capable, willing, and able to fulfill their duties. The sponsor does not guarantee successful outcomes but instead serves as the informed "gatekeeper" who ensures that the retirement products offered to participants deliver the promised services. Of course, the regulator is essential too, but I see the regulator more as setting the tone for the industry and monitoring the fiduciaries than as interacting directly with the end-consumer.

Finally, for a plan to be both effective and feasible, we need to make efficient use of all available assets, have low-cost fees and services, engage in continuing innovation, and ensure that the plan (1) has a defined-contribution (DC) legal structure to control cost and limit balance sheet risk to the plan sponsor and (2) is portable.

Simple for the Consumer: A Learning-by-Doing User Interface That Never Changes

In a "keep it simple for the consumer" system, all the consumer might see is a single page on a screen with choices and the necessary information to make those choices. That page has the person's target income per year (think Jane Austen), which is the amount that allows him to achieve the goal of a proper retirement. He is also given some measure of the chance of reaching that goal, which is conveyed in a simple, intuitive fashion—for example, as a speedometer or dial representing a single probability number for success in achieving the goal. The screen shows a minimum income (a floor) that is very, very close to certain but not guaranteed. The only other pieces of information on the consumer's page are the contribution rate, how much is being saved, and the consumer's retirement date. That's it. What's obviously missing is any type of return (historical or projected) and the consumer's asset allocation. Rates of return available in the market and asset allocation are *important* factors in achieving success but are not *meaningful* information for consumer choice. The presentation really is, or should be, that simple.

Suppose an individual is looking at this simplified "dashboard" and sees his target income with a 60% chance of success. Like the high cholesterol number, that chance of success is not good news in terms of reaching his goal. So, what can he do about it? Only three actions can improve his lot—save more, work longer, or take more risk. Those are thus the only three decisions the consumer needs to think about in the context of retirement. And they are meaningful choices because if he increases his savings, his paycheck is going to be smaller. If he decides to work longer, he is going to have to keep carrying "those bricks" longer than he had planned and explain that decision to his significant others. Asking him highly technical questions such as "How much debt versus equity do you want?" or "How much exposure to large-cap European stocks do you want?" is a little bit like his going to buy a car and having the car salesman ask him what compression ratio in the engine he wants. He might know that a high compression ratio must be good, but how many people can convert a compression ratio into miles per gallon, into how much faster they'll get from 0 to 60 miles per hour, or into how much more reliable the car will be than some other car with a lower ratio? Miles per gallon, speed, reliability—these are the factors that the car buyer really cares about.

However, whereas provision of simple answers to these important questions may be what the consumer wants, providing those answers is not simple for either the producer or the regulator. As with your car, not all of the engineering is transparent to the consumer. If you were to drive a 1955 car, the accelerator would feel exactly the same to your foot as it does in a new car today. Of course, in 1955, the accelerator was connected to pieces of metal that then made the carburetor open. Today, all the connections are electronic, and you *could* activate them with your finger. Car manufacturers kept the pedal to make us comfortable because we know how to drive a car when we push the accelerator with our foot. How would you like it if you bought your next car and the accelerator was a button? Suppose you got in and were looking for a steering wheel and found it was a joystick instead. Think about that when you drive home tonight. The design for the consumer should be not only simple but also something that consumers are comfortable with using to minimize the learning effort. At the other extreme would be to expect the consumer to understand and make decisions about all the investment steps needed to get to his goal. In effect, it would be like dumping all of the car parts in the driveway and leaving them with a handbook for assembly that says, "After you put the car together, if it doesn't work, it's your problem."

These perspectives lead us to the complex part that relates to the issue of consumer protection and consumer education. The traditional way most people are told to look at their investments is in terms of accumulated wealth at retirement; sometimes there is a specific wealth goal called "The Number." Your 401(k) statements, for example, are required to show you how much your account went up or down in value. And when this wealth is reported in terms of the potential income it can generate, the reporting is almost always done by mechanically applying an annuity formula with an assumed fixed interest rate and a known life expectancy, as if there were no uncertainty about future interest rates. This simple transformation does not take into account the difference in risk between wealth and income, which is affected by real interest rates, inflation, and longevity—all factors that are, in fact, subject to considerable uncertainty.

To demonstrate the considerable difference between wealth and income goals, consider a hypothetical 45-year-old individual whose goal is a specific level of retirement income for life that starts at age 65. To simplify the analysis, let's assume for the illustration that we know for certain she will live to age 85. The safe, risk-free asset today in terms of this objective function is an inflation-protected deferred annuity that makes no payouts for 20 years and then pays the same amount (adjusted for inflation) each year for 20 years. Suppose she has enough money in her retirement account to buy that deferred annuity today. We would send her a note: "Congratulations, you've made it to Nirvana. We bought this security today to lock in your goal income, to avoid any risk of not getting the income you need for a good retirement. You have the risk-free asset." Next, we send her monthly or quarterly statements showing her retirement portfolio holdings and other standard information. **Figure 1** plots the monthly returns from 2003 to 2011 for the deferred annuity—created from a long-dated, U.S. TIPS (Treasury Inflation-Protected Securities) portfolio—measured in terms of both its market value in wealth units (dollars) and its value in income units.

In the traditional ways of measuring risk and return in terms of change in value, Panel A of Figure 1 shows what she sees as the returns on her risk-free asset. Upon inspection, the value of the deferred annuity fluctuates enormously, looking not at all like a risk-free asset, even though the income it will provide in retirement does not change at all. Thus, we have a huge communication problem about what is risky and what is safe arising from the standard reporting practice—a problem that is further compounded because we can't talk to the mass of people covered in these plans and they do not have financial

Figure 1. Measuring Risk Properly: Wealth vs. Income— Deferred Annuity Monthly Returns, February 2003–June 2011

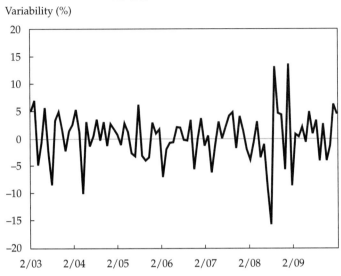

A. U.S. Dollar Return

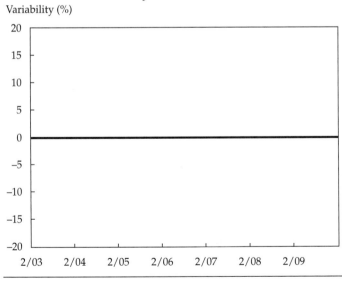

B. Annuity Income Unit Return

advisers. If we report the returns in income units, then the annuity does not fluctuate at all because its payments are exactly matched to the goal, as we see in Panel B. But the difficulty doesn't stop there.

A second challenge is regulators, who, with all good intent for consumer protection, feel the need to require minimum or guaranteed returns on the portfolio value. They want to make such investments safer for people because these accounts are core to funding their retirement income. Regulators have expressed interest in providing consumer protection by establishing a rule that consumers can at least be assured of getting their principal back—a floor, in other words. Some suggest not only a floor but also a minimum return—2 or 3%, for example—which, of course, can't even be achieved if the risk-free rate is lower—for instance, 1%. Remember, however, Jane Austen. The goal is income for life, protected from inflation, starting at retirement age—and not a goal of a target amount of wealth. So, it is retirement income uncertainty, not portfolio value, that is the true risk for consumers, and thus if such regulatory floors were to be established, they would need to be specified in terms of the safety of the income stream, not in terms of the market value of that stream. Volatility as risk should be measured in income units and not in value units.

As we see in Figure 1, Panel B, the deferred annuity is the safe asset, but under a proposed law with a floor on value of the portfolio, we could not provide this safe asset to consumers because if interest rates go up high enough, the price of the annuity could fall below the principal amount invested in the portfolio and would thus violate the proposed law. Ironically, legislation, or rules, intended to provide consumer protection and safety would have the clearly unintended consequence of not permitting the consumer to hold the risk-free asset. With all good intent, if consumer protection and safety is framed in the wrong units, unintended consequences can occur—regulations created that are actually counter to the public interest—and we might not know it until it is too late.

A third related challenge is deciding on the appropriate measure of risk and return to use for the goal selected. As shown in Panel B of Figure 1, if we measure returns in income units, which are the relevant units for our consumer, the variability we report each month will be flat. The point is that if we assess the investment in the right risk dimension, we get the right answer—namely, the annuity investment is very low risk in terms of the income goal.

As a further illustration to underscore this point, imagine a Japanese individual investing in the United States. Would we report U.S. dollar returns to this investor, or would he prefer to have yen returns reported? Does anybody over the last year doubt whether it would have made a difference?

Let's look at a more familiar asset, U.S. Treasury bills (T-bills), which are commonly treated as the risk-free asset. Panel A of **Figure 2** shows that, over eight years, the dollar returns to T-bills have been stable and principal has been

Figure 2. **Measuring Risk Properly: Wealth vs. Income—U.S. Three-Month T-Bill Monthly Returns, February 2003–June 2011**

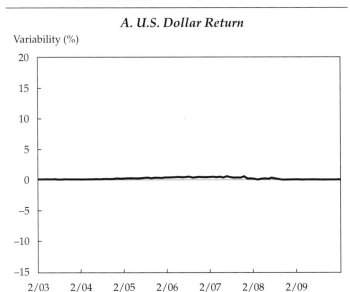

A. U.S. Dollar Return

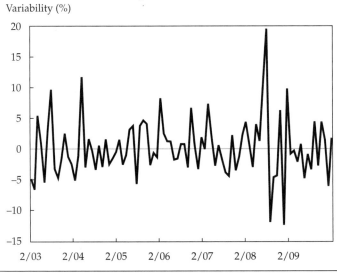

B. Annuity Income Unit Return

fully protected. But if we convert returns to the unit of measure that matters to our consumer, the annuity income unit, which Panel B of Figure 2 shows, then, T-bills are shown to be very risky and indeed nearly as volatile as the stock market.

To see what that volatility means in commonsense terms, consider a person who lives off his income from bank certificate of deposits and who has $1 million. At one time, not too long ago, he received 4%–5%, around $40,000–$50,000 a year in income, but now he is lucky to get 0.50%, $5,000 a year. Yes, the $1 million principal amount was fully insured and protected, but you can see he cannot remotely live on the amount received now. Furthermore, there is no reason to believe that these low interest rates are "temporary." Indeed, the U.S. Treasury term structure would seem to indicate otherwise. The CDs and U.S. Treasury bills preserve principal at all times but at the cost that the income received on them can vary enormously. Had he bought instead a long-maturity U.S. Treasury bond, his spendable income would be secure for the life of the bond, but the price of that bond would fluctuate substantially from day to day.

Figures 1 and 2 serve to demonstrate that when measuring risk and what is risk free, one must choose between a value frame of reference and an income frame. U.S. Treasury bills are indeed the risk-free asset if wealth preservation is the objective; in this scenario, annuities and long-duration U.S. Treasury bonds are very risky. If, however, preserving a secure stream of income over long periods of time, as in retirement, is the objective, then annuities and long-duration U.S. Treasury bonds become the risk-free asset and U.S. Treasury bills are very risky. It is not feasible to have both income preservation and capital preservation be risk free, although, of course, a mixed goal of both income and wealth preservation can lead to trade-offs between the risk of income versus wealth.

On this same point, **Figure 3**, with the familiar risk–return properties, shows the average return and volatility of three assets, U.S. Treasury bills, the inflation-protected lifetime annuity, and the MSCI World stock portfolio—measured in Panel A in the standard format in terms of wealth ($) and measured in Panel B in terms of income units. The risk and return information is based on data from February 2003 through June 2011. As Figure 3 shows, whether we measure and report the risk–return character of assets in wealth versus annuity income units gives quite different pictures, especially with respect to U.S. Treasury bills and the annuity. This implies that allocation among various asset classes can be materially affected. Presenting the information in the wrong format for the chosen goal can be incredibly misleading. In fact, if combined with regulations and rules that are also imposed on the wrong measures, the result can be dysfunctional.

Even a simple change, such as showing annuity values in units of the annuity, can be complex. How do we codify it properly in regulations? How do we educate the gatekeepers and producers? This industry is huge; billions of

Figure 3.   Managing the Risk–Return Trade-Off Properly: Wealth vs. Income

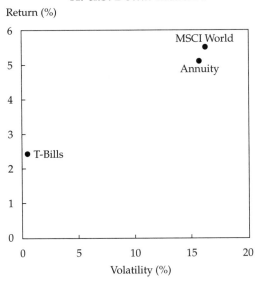

A. U.S. Dollar Measure

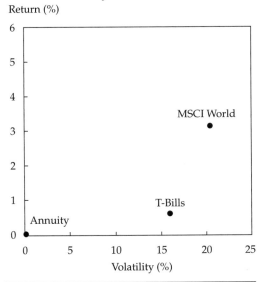

B. Annuity Income Unit Measure

Note: Based on data for February 2003–June 2011.

dollars are invested in various computer models of risk and return and optimal asset allocation. The bad news is that the users and producers of these models have invested huge resources, financial and training, in creating and purchasing them, and they are not likely to want to scrap them for something completely different. But the good news is that they do not need to change their models. They only have to change the units in which they measure the return characteristics of the various asset classes from one of $ to one of income units. This is no more challenging than making a change of currency in which returns are denominated and then applying the same models as before.

Earlier, I mentioned the importance of *integration* of all the assets dedicated to funding retirement, and not just the DC account, when determining optimal asset allocation for the DC account. What's relevant to the retirement problem is not just the assets the individual is investing today, or even her Social Security or other plan assets. The individual's future contributions are an integral part of retirement planning, particularly when individuals are young and most of their retirement assets are in the form of future contributions. Future contributions are not only a large retirement asset in amount but also a rather low-risk asset, more like a bond than stocks. Indeed, the goal of retirement is not a fixed amount of income but, instead, a replacement ratio. That is, to sustain a standard of living based on a high income requires a higher amount of income in retirement than it does for a low income. So, if one lives on a $50,000 income while working, perhaps 70% of the income is needed in retirement to sustain that standard of living because there is no longer a need to save. Then, the goal becomes $35,000. However, if the person's income while working increases to $70,000, the new target income goal for retirement becomes $49,000. If, instead, income declines to $40,000, the income in retirement also falls to $28,000. Thus, contributions that are typically proportional to income get larger when more is needed and get smaller when less is needed instead of remaining rigid, as would be the case for a bond. In that sense, the future contributions may be more of a hedge and less risky relative to the goal than a U.S. Treasury bond.

Optimal asset allocation is not only age related but also based on level of income and amount of accumulation and current market conditions for both equities and real interest rates. To illustrate this point, **Table 1** looks at three people, most likely of different ages, with the same total value of retirement assets, the same overall asset allocation between equities and fixed income, but different distributions of that total asset value between the DC account and future contributions. Table 1 also shows the meaningful measures of the riskiness of their future contribution assets. Considering all the assets of each individual, including the future contributions, the total value for each of them is $1,000. All three individuals' investments are allocated 70% in fixed income and 30% in equities. Individual A is obviously much younger than the other

Table 1. An Integrated Retirement Investment Approach to Asset Allocation

Individual	Total Assets	FC/SS/DB	DC Pension Amount	DC Pension Ratio
Individual A				
Total	$1,000	$700	$300	
Fixed income	700	700	0	0%
Equity	300	0	300	100
Individual B				
Total	$1,000	$500	$500	
Fixed income	700	500	200	33%
Equity	300	0	300	67
Individual C				
Total	$1,000	$100	$900	
Fixed income	700	100	600	67%
Equity	300	0	300	33

Note: FC is future contributions, SS is Social Security benefits, DB is defined-benefit plan income, and DC is defined-contribution pension.

two (or hasn't had such good results in the market) because 70% of the value of that person's retirement assets is in future contributions and only 30% is in financial assets. If this person wants to get a 30/70 equity/fixed allocation for all his retirement assets, he would need to invest 100% of his DC account in equities, which is a risky position. If this individual had been 100% in equities in September 2008, by March 2009, he would have had between a 35% and 40% loss in his account. Pretty bad. But remember that this investment is only 30%, not 100%, of his total retirement assets. In this case, the individual's total retirement assets are not down 40%; they are down 40% on 30% or 12% overall, which is not great but is certainly better than down 40%.

Individual B is probably older, closer to mid-career, than Individual A and, as shown in the second and third columns of Table 1, has relatively more financial assets: $500 versus $700 for FC/SS/DB and $500 versus $300 for DC pension. To achieve the same overall asset allocation of 30/70, this person would need to be invested one-third in fixed income and two-thirds in equities in his DC account.

Individual C, who is (depending on her experience) probably five to eight years from retirement, has 90% of her retirement assets in the market and only 10% in expected future contributions. She optimally holds only one-third of her DC assets in equities.

This example shows that apparent systemically increasing investment conservatism with age need not reflect changes in risk aversion. Rather, with increasing age, the relatively safer future-contribution retirement asset is becoming a smaller portion of overall retirement assets as the person moves forward toward retirement.

Table 1 demonstrates how different the optimal asset allocations between equities and fixed income are for the DC account, even though the total asset portfolio risk is identical for all three. As we see, trying to achieve an optimal asset allocation for the DC account without taking these other assets into account may be unrealistic. These distinctions lead us, again, to consumer protection.

Regulations and oversight are appropriate—particularly given that DC plans are now going to be the core, not the supplementary, retirement vehicle globally for great masses of people. But we must educate our gatekeepers—the plan producers, plan sponsors, consultants, and regulators—not only about the appropriate measures of risk and return but also about the integrated view of consumers' sources of retirement income. In this way, we can set the appropriate rules and regulations right from the outset, rather than having to correct or reverse them later on, which is always more difficult.

Future Innovations: Education and Financial Instruments

In terms of consumer financial education, we have to be realistic about what we can expect people to understand (or what they should have to understand). I believe we should not try to force financial education on plan participants, whether brain surgeons, professors, or auto assembly line workers. For one thing, they don't want to learn it. People generally do not enjoy doing personal finance. For example, a family member of mine is a brilliant woman, a successful professional, and at retirement age. She hates having to deal with all this financial business; for her, it's like going to the dentist and having her teeth fixed without Novocain. And it's not that she doesn't understand money; she just doesn't like doing personal finance.

We can make smart consumers, however, by creating products that make them smart rather than by literally educating them. Intelligent product design and oversight can be an effective substitute for consumer financial education. Such products can also be designed to offset, rather than change, financially dysfunctional behavior, which is well-documented. Of course, this approach is not easy for the developers of financial products, regulators, and plan sponsors. But they have to take on the complex job of making investing for retirement income simple for the consumer. Not only are developments in user-interface design required, but also innovation is a key component in solving these consumer problems and financial education challenges.

The technology and the mathematical tools needed to carry out much of the innovation in plan design are already available and have been market-tested in other applications. Insurance companies and pension funds already conduct dynamic immunization trading to replicate the payoffs to a fixed-income instrument that hedges the risks of their liability exposures—often referred to as "liability-driven investing." This kind of immunization strategy needs to be employed in each individual's account, where the "liability" is the individual's specific income goal needed to sustain her standard of living. It cannot, however, be done with a simple mutual fund or with a static mix of stocks and bonds in a portfolio. It has to be done, if it's going to be done seriously and professionally, by people with the skills to do it at low cost and with the appropriate degree of precision. It requires that each individual not have segregated ownership of the account but that the account be managed for her as an individual and not in a pooled fund in which everyone of the same age has the same investments and thus implicitly the same income goal in retirement, independent of gender or income level.

As an illustration, most people would not want to buy an actual life annuity during the accumulation period prior to retirement as a means to insure against interest rate and longevity risks. Instead, the typical individual would prefer to buy tradable assets, such as TIPS and longevity bonds, that hedge the cost of buying an annuity when retirement is reached. If the individual buys an annuity on his life, it's reversible only at a high cost, which means if he dies two years from now, he loses everything. If his life circumstances change—get married, get divorced, start a second family—the lack of flexibility can be costly. The right time for him to determine the detail of post-retirement investment choices (including either immediate or deferred life annuity to protect against the risk of outliving his assets, income ladders, working for five years and allowing Social Security benefits to grow before drawing on them, and so forth) is as close to retirement as possible when he has the most information about his health, his responsibilities, his opportunities, and his preferences.

But to make sure that the individual has the necessary resources to implement that post-retirement plan, the investment strategy during accumulation should hedge the risk that he will have enough money to buy that insurance when he retires. That can be done with TIPS for interest rate risk and a generic longevity bond on the cohort in which he will be placed by insurance companies in determining the price they will charge for the annuity—an instrument based on broad characteristics, such as age, birth date, gender, geography, or whatever is useful. The point is to have a tradable, reversible instrument not linked to a specific individual's mortality but to the cohort in which that individual belongs. That product can be created in many ways, but unfortunately, the markets have not yet developed as much as they will have to. Innovation is needed.

Which brings me to securitization. Did that go awry during the Great Financial Crisis of 2008–2009? Absolutely. But we will need a revitalization of securitization if we are to tackle the retirement challenge in the right way. In particular, a well-designed and efficiently priced reverse mortgage is likely to be an important means for working- and middle-class retirees to achieve a good retirement. Placing the risk of these mortgages with the best holders of that risk will require securitization. To demonize or regulate away the ability to innovate new financial products that will be instrumental in addressing our key retirement challenges would be bad policy that we cannot afford.

Some further innovations that I think should be considered for individual employees' retirement plans are listed below:

- integration to include other retirement-dedicated assets, including rollover IRAs from previous employment, after-tax dedicated personal savings, and house as both a prepaid consumption and a retirement-funding asset;

- bequest and housing asset-use efficiency: well-designed reverse mortgage;

- longevity bonds, swaps, and other cohort-based, tradable, longevity-hedging instruments;

- product efficiency: combine long-term care and life annuity to reduce the distortion of selection bias in both products' pricing;

- age-, means-, and interest-rate-dependent employer contribution rates to reduce participant duration-mismatch risk;

- products to address standard-of-living risk: consumption-linked income units;

- tail insurance on longevity: >85 life annuities.

Question and Answer Session

Question: I'm not sure the *riskless* asset exists as you've described it. I think we can talk about the *lowest-risk* asset, but an insurance company still has credit risk. And what about liquidity? Annuities exist in the market, but no one buys them because they want liquidity to deal with any eventualities.

Merton: When I said the "risk-free asset," I meant we should think of it as the lowest-risk asset—that's the spirit I mean it in. I'm trying to convey that real interest rate risk, inflation risk, and longevity risk exist. And the norm, if you look at some of the so-called glide paths on target date funds, is to glide people into T-bills when they turn 65, which I have shown is actually very risky if retirement income is the goal. Not every plan producer does that anymore, but some still do.

With regard to credit risk, we should be aware of potential default risk for insurance companies. Having said that, as far as I know, there have not been any defaults on insurance company annuities or situations in which state insurance guarantee funds have had to step in to prevent a default. It could, of course, happen, but a whole bunch of other risks are out there to which there is no precise solution.

There is an answer to the risks, however, and it is a quantitative answer. In the simplest terms, cutting out all of the expenses, a person reaches 65 and is willing to buy an annuity at the best cost out there. To get rid of as many frictions as we can, we would want a real annuity. And we have them; real annuities exist. If, for example, real interest rates are 2%, then a life annuity will offer you a payout of about 6% for the rest of your life—even if you live to 120. That $6 - 2 = 4\%$ additional "mortality credit," a greater than market interest rate payout while alive in return for giving up your investment principal at death when you no longer need it, is an enormous difference in payout that most people will not have the luxury of forgoing. That's why addressing the credit risk of annuities is a big policy issue.

Question: You talked about designing financial products in a way that makes it less necessary for the consumer to understand the product. I think there's a big assumption underneath that idea, which is that the financial business has integrity. Without a savvy consumer base, how do you take care of the situation in which producers mislead people intentionally?

Merton: That's a good question because it gives me a chance to clarify what I thought I said. I'd like to make two points. First, a lot is going on that consumers won't be able to understand. You can give them all the data and information in the world, but they're not going to be able to make an informed decision any more than if you were to show them x-ray films and ask them to make a judgment about some complex surgery. There are, however, choices that consumers should be the ones to make.

On the one hand, if they're wheeling me into surgery, I don't want the surgeon to say, "Mr. Merton, do you want 12 or 17 sutures?" He's being completely transparent with me, but he's scared the heck out of me. His question makes me think that he doesn't know and that he expects me to give him an expert technical answer.

On the other hand, if I'm getting a hip or knee replacement and the doctor says, "Look, you can get the standard one; it's very safe, not too expensive, and not too painful. But you will not be able to jog. Or you can get the sports one that's much more expensive; it's painful, and there are more risks involved, but you'll be able to jog when you're 90." That is a meaningful choice for me, the consumer, because the consumer knows whether the expensive one is worth it or not, depending on whether his life revolves around running.

The second point relates to oversight. The consumer can learn some basics, but a more plausible approach is a governance or oversight structure in which the gatekeeper is not the individual but the plan sponsor. The plan sponsor has the resources, has a shared responsibility as a fiduciary with the consumer, and can do the oversight on behalf of its employees. I have a lot of commercial evidence—I don't do academic research on this issue—that, believe it or not, people trust their employers. They trust their employers more than they trust banks, more than they trust the government, more than they trust a whole bunch of other people.

So, let's put that responsibility—and have complete transparency—on the one who can evaluate plans and understand them and has fiduciary responsibility and good rapport with the consumers. If the plan sponsor does not have the oversight, then perhaps the plan should be carried out by another, similarly trusted and more capable, entity.

What is unreasonable is expecting that even highly educated people with very high IQs can evaluate these complex financial choices. There are, of course, good rules of thumb to help the consumer—for example, "markets are efficient." You may say, "Oh, that's a bad one," because it is not entirely empirically valid. Where do efficient markets come from? What's the concept basically? "No free lunch," right? That's the kind of rule of thumb we can teach people: Namely, when something's too good to be true, it likely is not true. We have to be realistic about what is useful and meaningful to teach people for this important activity.

Question: If we take your descriptors of the choices that we want consumers to make—target income, contribution rate, and so on—it sounds as if one of the things you're asking the regulator to do is to translate fairly or accurately the characteristics of the product into the choices we're asking the consumers to make. So, to go back to your hip replacement example, when the surgeon is offering the choice "you can have this one that's inexpensive and moderately painful, and then there's another one that's more expensive but you'll be able to run when you're 90," don't you want the regulator to be able to, in effect, vet that description to be sure that it is accurate? So, when we're comparing products in terms of the five or six characteristics that we identify, does the regulator have to enforce the translation from the complex product attributes to the simple descriptors from which the consumer would be choosing, to be sure that the characterizations are accurate?

Merton: That's correct, but I want to clarify that, as in my example, it doesn't literally mean that the regulator must always examine for suitability and reliability each particular element, product, or strategy. The regulator may instead impose that the plan sponsor, as a fiduciary, and its consultant perform that role. And if the plan sponsor fails at this role, then the plan sponsor will be held accountable for that failure.

Question: You're putting a lot of responsibility on the plan sponsor, who's not necessarily an expert because plan sponsors vary in size.

Merton: We have an answer that fits each situation, but it's not necessarily the same answer. For example, for large plan sponsors who have consultants—who are now fiduciaries, in my understanding of the rule—the regulator need not go door to door and examine every element directly. In other situations, that task may be the right answer. For smaller plan sponsors, who do not have the resources, there can be regular approved "safe-harbor" strategies that are not costly to comply with. What doesn't make sense to me is handing people a handbook and saying, "You solve it."

Either the plan sponsor or someone else for whom we set requirements should be responsible. It's similar to the case of risk bearing. Individuals are bearing risks, such as inherent, structural interest rate risk (like a bank bears), that they should not have to bear.

I'll give you a simple example. When you participate in a DC plan, one of the first risks you have, even in the simplest world, is enormous interest rate risk. Suppose you are just starting your work life and you're going to earn a sure income (wouldn't that be nice!) for the rest of your life. You have no money accumulated, but you're going to save, say, 8% of your income each year. You put in 8% this year, 8% next year, 8%, 8%, and so on. Then what? You start taking it out. Do you see the timing? The first amount out comes after the last amount in. Inherently and structurally, you have a huge duration mismatch—that is, your payouts and your pay-ins are not matched in time. Therefore, if interest rates change, you're at risk. Every single person who participates in a DC plan faces that risk.

We could say, "Well, that's life. Let them bear it." But that doesn't make sense. A better solution would be to change the contributions. No one ordained that it had to be 8%. Why not make the contributions a function of interest rates? When you're short duration, you come out ahead when interest rates go up, and you come out behind when interest rates go down. Employer contributions would go down when interest rates go up—instead of 8%, let's say 7.9%, for example—and contributions would go up when interest rates go down. We've now shifted at least some of that inherent structural interest rate risk away from every individual in the plan.

That's the spirit of what I'm calling for. I don't pretend that I can prescribe how exactly to do it with regulators, but there's always going to be a better way to do this sort of thing.

Question: If I buy an investment from my plan sponsor that is supposed to provide a certain probability of achieving a given level of real income, or if I buy it from some consultant that he's hired, how do I verify that they're actually doing the right thing? Here I am at 40, it's supposed to pay off at 65, and I have to trust this provider for 25 years?

Merton: We can't get around this problem. Defined-benefit plans are held out as an example of a guaranteed return, but they aren't really, not just because the corporation can fail but because the plans are so back-loaded. When you're a young person with 25 or 30 years until retirement, the DB promise is small, but if you're still there in 25–30 years, the promise is big. People ask, "Why can't you guarantee it to me?" But nobody can guarantee an income *replacement ratio*. No insurance company can, and nobody else can. In addition, if I quoted you a price, you wouldn't like it. When they consider interest rates, most people find that they've got to take some risk rather than save 70% of their income, or whatever big number they would have to save, to get absolute security.

Who should be evaluating that need for risk taking? The individual? Or the three parties I mentioned earlier: the plan sponsor, the regulator, and the provider—all of whom have some responsibility? Yes, the individual can cross-insure to mitigate credit risk, but credit risk isn't the only risk. As I mentioned in my remarks, is anybody actually getting a meaningful part of her income from certificates of deposit today? People for years were getting 4% or 5%, but today, they are getting 0.3% if they're lucky. They have their principal absolutely protected; we did a perfect job of providing capital preservation with deposit insurance. But we insured them against the wrong risk. They were protected against credit risk, but they ended up with something that did much more damage to them, income risk from changing interest rates.

Question: The three factors that people need to make decisions about are how much risk they are willing to take, how long they plan to keep working, and how much money they have to put away. Have you done any experimental work to see how people make decisions about those three things? I'm concerned about people thinking that they can work forever, whereas physically maybe they can't, or choosing large amounts of risk that they may come to regret later.

Merton: I haven't done formal, large-sample research on this issue because it's not my area of expertise. What I have done is a lot of work with focus groups, with real clients, to try to figure out how people react to various pieces of information and questions, to see what works. Anecdotally, with the proper framing of choices and easy-to-use tools to execute them, for the most part, people end up doing the right thing. (As an aside, it's most important that people make the right decisions, but sometimes, we get too focused on the process.) They understand the issues, even if not all the underlying finance. Furthermore, what's important is not that they get the decisions precisely right, because the world changes all the time, but that they have the right mindset. With that and the right tools, people can get into the habit of checking if they are on track and if not, taking steps to get back on track. They play with the tools to see if things get better if they save a little bit more or work a bit longer, and they get to know the process and the impact of changing the inputs. They do all this without a handbook. It can become a routine. If people never get involved, however, you, the professional, have to manage their money the best you can for them, setting sensible goals for retirement and executing dynamic asset management to do the best you can to get them there.

Opening Remarks: Duke

Research, Policy, and the Future of Financial Education

Elizabeth A. Duke
Governor
Board of Governors of the Federal Reserve System

I would like to thank Eric Rosengren, President of the Federal Reserve Bank of Boston, for inviting me to speak to you today. This is the third in a series of conferences on the Future of Life-Cycle Saving and Investing cosponsored by Boston University School of Management and the Boston Reserve Bank. The audience here includes leading academics in household finance and consumer financial education, industry practitioners, and policymakers. The work you do every day is critically important to the financial well-being of American consumers and to the overall functioning of our economy.

Today's topic is a daunting one: how to improve consumers' financial education. I hope to set the stage for your discussions by sharing my perspective on recent economic factors and trends in the financial services industry and the impact they have had on consumers, particularly those with low and moderate incomes. I will also give you my thoughts on the role of financial education in facilitating effective decision making and suggest areas where additional research could help shape policies and practices to benefit individual consumers and lead to safe and sustainable economic growth.

The Case for Financial Education

I certainly do not need to impress upon this audience the importance of financial education. Today's consumers are making decisions among increasingly complex financial products and in the context of uncertain economic times. A working knowledge of basic financial terms and concepts can lead to better economic decisions and outcomes for individuals over the course of a lifetime. In addition, there is a clear relationship between *individuals'* financial decisions and the health of our entire economy.

The financial crisis and the slow recovery from it have obviously had a dramatic impact on the financial decisions made by American families. Many now have fewer financial resources and limited options. The pace and timing of their saving and investing life cycle have also been disrupted. For example, high unemployment levels among recent high school and college graduates, especially among young African Americans, means that this demographic likely may not be able to start saving and investing as early in life as previous generations.

In addition, starting salaries for recent college graduates have also declined, which means that young Americans who *are* employed will have fewer resources for saving and investing than their predecessors. Young people are living with their parents longer, which helps conserve their limited resources but likely places a strain on their parents' budgets.

Also troubling is research showing that many consumers who should be *saving* for retirement instead have been forced to take hardship withdrawals from their 401(k) plans. According to an analysis by Vanguard, hardship withdrawals increased by 49% between 2005 and 2010. Other types of withdrawals increased by 56%.

The increasing use of retirement savings for other purposes is particularly troubling given that the responsibility for saving for retirement has shifted away from employers to individual employees. Having a secure retirement is a high priority and a significant long-term goal for many Americans, so it is especially important that they have an understanding of what level of resources they will need in retirement and the investment options available to them.

Individuals who are approaching retirement age, in particular, are being forced to make changes to their plans for retirement. Social Security Administration data indicate that in 2009 and 2010, the proportions of men and women claiming Social Security benefits at age 62 began to rise again after several years of decline. Workers have either chosen to leave the work force early in the last few years or, more likely, have applied for Social Security benefits as early as possible because of the weak job market.[1] Opting to receive a smaller Social Security annuity earlier in life is just one of many hard decisions Americans have had to make in order to balance their short-term and long-term financial needs.

The recession has clearly disrupted the future expectations and financial plans of millions of Americans, but even in the best of circumstances, effectively managing one's longevity risk requires a level of financial knowledge well beyond that required of any previous generation. The pending retirement of Baby Boomers means that millions of older households will need to assess pension distributions and make decisions about payout options for their defined benefit plans. Those with defined contribution plans will need to make decisions about the purchase of annuities or rates of withdrawal from these plans.

---

[1]In 2004, 50% of men and 54% of women were new retirement beneficiaries at age 62. These percentages dropped to 42% for men and 48% for women (i.e., both men and women were staying in the labor force longer) through 2008; in 2009 and 2010, these proportions rose again, to 43.6% and 49.0%, respectively. Social Security Administration Annual Statistical Supplement, 2007 and 2010, Table 6.B1.

Younger workers, a majority of whom will not have pensions, will need to make complicated decisions about their target amounts of retirement savings, portfolio allocation, and asset management using 401(k) plans, individual retirement accounts, and other non-tax-advantaged accounts.

Financial products have also become more complex, adding a significant degree of difficulty to the important task of managing one's own retirement savings. Consumers need information and education to understand their saving and investment options, to make the best choices for themselves and their families, and to help them implement and monitor these choices over time.

In short, your efforts to identify, address, and meet the financial education needs of consumers in all stages of the life cycle have never been more urgent.

Changing Consumer Behaviors and Information Needs

The financial crisis has changed all of our assumptions about the future. Naturally, consumer behavior is changing as a result, although it is unclear whether these changes represent temporary or more permanent shifts in thinking and planning for the future.

For example, the collapse of housing prices and resulting worker immobility has changed consumers' appetite for homeownership. In Fannie Mae's 2010 Own-Rent Analysis, the percentage of respondents who said they were more likely to rent their next home than buy climbed from 30% in January to 33% in December of the same year.

Similarly, the recent increase in gasoline prices has affected consumer choices in housing and other purchases, big and small. Family incomes have not kept pace with rising costs, and many families, particularly those with low-to-moderate incomes, are actually facing the decision between buying gas to drive long distances to work and paying their mortgage. During the housing boom, when gas prices were much lower, potential homebuyers moved steadily farther away from employment centers in search of more affordable homes. This was referred to as the "drive till you qualify" method of home buying. Foreclosures remain high in these areas where the cost of driving to work has become so great.

But even independent of recent economic trends and the increasing complexity of financial products, consumers' need for financial information and education is changing.

Evolving Education Needs

There is growing evidence that the changing financial services landscape has disconnected young and other vulnerable consumers from mainstream financial services, making them more prone to using alternative financial products. For example, some consumers prefer using reloadable stored-value cards to opening a deposit account at a bank or credit union.[2] This choice could have significant implications for a consumer's financial well-being, both good and bad. These cards, with their Visa and MasterCard branding, make it easy for consumers to make purchases online but do not carry the same robust federal protections as debit or credit cards, and their use does not establish a relationship with a financial institution that can serve as the entry point for other financial services, such as loans.

As more and more new products are introduced to the financial marketplace, it becomes more important for consumers to be able to evaluate and compare products' benefits and potential costs. Many consumers seek the advice of friends and family when making financial decisions. Online social networks are increasingly playing this role as a source of financial information, particularly among younger consumers.[3] At the same time, it is crucial that they also have access to accurate, comprehensive, and unbiased financial information.

Starting Financial Education Early

Successfully navigating the volumes of financial information out there, whether from advertisements, advisers, or social media, requires critical skills based on a foundation of numeracy, language arts, and decision making that is first developed in school. It is important that these skills be included in curriculum and measured in student achievement tests. If our schools cannot spare the resources to provide financial literacy as a subject unto itself, I believe that the concepts required for sound financial decision making should, at a minimum, be incorporated into existing subject areas. Math problems can involve consumer financial calculations. Social studies classes can help students understand the real-world financial issues and decisions they will face as young adults. I also think that the work many of you are doing to make financial lessons more appealing to school-aged children is extremely important given the competition for attention from media and web-based entertainment and games.

More broadly, financial education is a life-long endeavor. Sound financial decisions are made when consumers have access to information that is clear and culturally relevant and that is provided at critical "teachable" moments, such as when a consumer is financing education, buying a car, starting a family, purchasing a house, or planning for retirement. These are just a few examples. As academicians, practitioners, and policymakers, we need to identify as many of these moments as possible and determine how best to support positive financial outcomes for consumers at those moments.

---

[2]Corey Stone and Joshua Sledge, "Financial First Encounters: An Examination of the Fractured Financial Landscape Facing Youth Today," Center for Financial Services Innovation (2010).

[3]Wendy Way, Nancy Wong, and Constance Steinkuehler, "Social Network Sites and Internet Forums: An Investigation of Interactions around Personal Finance in the Online Social World," University of Wisconsin–Madison (2010).

Reaching Consumers

There is a saying among communications professionals that "the medium *is* the message." In that vein, I believe that how we deliver financial education has a significant impact on how effective the lessons will be. New technologies present exciting new opportunities to deliver timely financial lessons. Mobile payments and financial services are growing at a rapid pace.[4] Financial management "apps" for smart phones abound, making it possible for consumers to get just-in-time information. The developments in mobile financial services have only begun to exploit the potential of this technology to provide tools for consumer financial decision making. I will be particularly interested to see how technology can be used to better serve lower-income populations who may be more focused on stretching their paychecks to meet monthly expenses than on investing. If you can have an app to track what you eat, certainly you could use one to track what you spend.

Evaluating the Effectiveness of Financial Education

Until now, we have had a limited understanding of which methods work best with respect to financial education. For years, one of the correlates of higher scores on the Jump$tart Financial Literacy test was participation in the Stock Market Game, an enrichment program offered in many schools. The FINRA Education Foundation sponsored a study to determine just what it was about the game that made a difference. Not surprisingly, the answer is that the game seems to develop math skills.[5]

Entertainment-based financial education also seems to be effective in capturing attention and instilling knowledge among youths. Young people who played one of the Doorways to Dreams (D2D) financial education games reported increases in financial knowledge, aspirations, and self-confidence.[6]

Among young adults, financial education was found to be most relevant when it was tied to financial outcomes.[7] For example, in a Federal Reserve study conducted with Army Emergency Relief, young enlisted service members who participated in a financial education program seemed to make better

---

[4]Mobile payments and financial services have grown nearly fivefold from 2007 to 2010, and that growth is projected to continue at about 20% per year over the next four years. Javelin Strategy and Research, "2010 Mobile Banking and Smartphone Forecast" (2010).

[5]Learning Point Associates, "The Stock Market Game Study: Brief Report" (2009).

[6]Financial entertainment games include Celebrity Calamity, Bite Club, Groove Nation, and Farm Blitz. Information on preliminary evaluations is available at www.d2dfund.org/financial_entertainment_preliminary_results.

[7]Joshua Sledge, Jennifer Tescher, and Sarah Gordon, "From Financial Education to Financial Capability: Opportunities for Innovation," Center for Financial Services Innovation (2010).

car-buying decisions. These soldiers had higher down payment-to-loan ratios and shorter-term loans than a comparison group who did not take the financial education program.[8]

These are notable examples, but the fact is that we have very limited data on how effective financial education is in improving financial well-being. The Financial Literacy and Education Commission, of which the Federal Reserve is a member, has only recently developed a core set of financial competencies and has yet to establish the knowledge, skills, and behaviors that will meet these competencies.

In order to develop an effective financial course of study, we need to find the answers to some important research questions. I believe the answers to these questions will be quite important:

- What do people need to know in order to improve their long-term economic well-being? How does this content vary across demographic groups, such as by income, employment status, age, or culture?

- How do people obtain and process financial information? What sources do they use? Do outcomes vary by the source or timing of the information?

- Is instilling financial knowledge enough to improve consumer outcomes, or do we need to fundamentally change consumer behavior as well? How can we as policymakers influence financial behaviors?

- How should financial literacy be measured to evaluate the impact of financial education on financial outcomes and predict future behavior and well-being? Should these measures vary across demographic groups and the context in which consumers make financial decisions?

Undoubtedly some of the research shared at this conference will shed light on these questions and also raise others. I look forward to learning from your work and to implementing and supporting programs that have demonstrated results.

Conclusion

Decisions about saving and investing have a profound effect on the financial well-being of individual consumers. Collectively, those same decisions shape our national economic outcomes. Changes in the financial products offered to consumers and in the economic circumstances of those consumers have added even more complexity to the financial decisions faced by consumers. Comprehensive, effective regulation of consumer products is the first step

---

[8]Catherine Bell and Jeanne M. Hogarth, "Better Deals on Wheels: The Effects of Financial Education on Car Buying," Federal Reserve Bank of Minneapolis, *Community Dividend* (April 2010). The Center for Financial Services Innovation also promotes relevance as one of the key features of innovative financial education programs.

in ensuring positive outcomes for consumers. But consumers must also be equipped with the necessary quantitative and decision-making tools, and supported with the right information at the right time in order to make the best possible choices. While much attention and many resources have been devoted to financial education, we still have surprisingly little information about the effectiveness of financial literacy efforts. I hope that the dialog facilitated by this conference and future research will focus on understanding the best who, what, when, where, and why of financial education that will help American consumers make better decisions and achieve better financial futures. The outcomes of this conference will help us develop the tools to do that. I commend you for your efforts and wish each of you success here and in the future.

Session 1: Consumer Finance 101 for Financial Educators, Financial Advisers, and Regulators

Panel Discussion

Zvi Bodie, Moderator
Norman and Adele Barron Professor of Management
Boston University

Stephen Horan, CFA, CIPM
Head, University Relations and Private Wealth
CFA Institute

John Gannon
Senior Vice President, Investor Education
President, FINRA Investor Education Foundation
Financial Industry Regulatory Authority (FINRA)

Peter Tufano
Peter Moores Dean, Saïd Business School
University of Oxford

Chris Farrell
Economics Editor
Marketplace Money

Stephen Horan

My perspective is specifically investor education. I will make three general points. First, we need to approach the issue of investor education with humility because there is a lot that we do not know about its efficacy. We have a great deal of research, and a lot of investor education is going on, but we do not know much about the outcome. Second, we need a sense of humility about what we think the goals should be and what the correct behavior for individuals really is. Third, we need to recognize the important issue of *numeracy*—the ability to work with numbers—and how it relates to the role of investment advice in investment education.

Information in the Marketplace. Competitive markets depend on quality information in order to function properly. Robert Merton argued convincingly at this conference that simplicity for the consumer means complexity for the producer (see Merton's piece in this book). I certainly agree. The drive for *apparent* simplicity, however, also creates obscurity for the consumer, resulting in a lack of transparency that has an implication for and an impact on how the market functions.

Consider how the costs of financial transactions have plummeted over the last couple of decades. Now, we can trade for $5 a trade, but the costs of financial products have not changed. A simple actively managed mutual fund costs about 1.45% per year, much as it has for decades. Our insurance products are priced similarly to what they were priced a decade or two ago. I think the reason is largely that quality information, information that can be easily digested by the consumer, is not available in the marketplace. This situation creates obscurity. Consumers, therefore, look to price as a signal of quality, so producers do not have an incentive to improve quality or to cut prices. This situation might be one where regulators could step in; they could provide incentives for innovation, for transparency, and for quality of information in the marketplace.

Finding Effective Investor Education. Investor education has a sketchy track record. Lauren Willis, who spoke at this conference (see Willis's piece in this book), has written what I consider to be a seminal paper on investor education.[1] She articulately laid out how complex the whole issue is. The marketplace has unobservable costs. A lot of biases and powerful incentives lie behind the educators.

We need to be careful about the conclusions we draw from the literature. When we examine—dig down into—the studies, we find enormous methodological problems. Something as simple as an experimental control group is missing in a strikingly large percentage of investor education studies. Use of a control group is part of basic scientific methodology. Other problems, such as selection bias and attribution bias, plague studies. Even the studies that are methodologically strong provide results that are fairly weak—sometimes, paradoxically. Mandell and Klein conducted a meta-analysis of studies of investor education students who took personal finance courses.[2] Ironically, the authors

---

[1]Lauren E. Willis, "Against Financial-Literacy Education," *Iowa Law Review*, vol. 94, no. 1 (November 2008):197–285.
[2]Lewis Mandell and Linda Schmid Klein, "The Impact of Financial Literacy Education on Subsequent Financial Behavior," *Journal of Financial Counseling and Planning*, vol. 20, no. 1 (2009):15–24.

found that these students did no better than people who did not take such a course and, in fact, actually did worse (although statistically insignificantly) than students who did not take a financial planning course.

Therefore, investor education runs the danger of creating overconfidence among investors and giving the illusion of effective education, the illusion of knowledge. The result is that people can actually make worse decisions than they might have otherwise.

We often create analogies between investment advice and legal advice or medical advice. The analogy is useful in helping to elevate the investment profession, but a more instructive, if more pedestrian, analogy is between investment advice and driver education—particularly, education on the inner workings of the car. The knowledge base required to drive a car and the knowledge base required to manage one's finances can be sorted into three categories:

1. the skills that everybody needs to have, no matter who they are. If they are going to be engaged in this activity, they need these skills.

2. an intermediate set of skills for those who are fairly robust in this particular field and reasonably choose to take on more-advanced tasks.

3. some highly advanced skills that really ought to be left to the experts.

At the first level in driver education, we can think about defensive driving skills, checking for flat tires, emergency responses on the road, what to do if the "Check Oil" light comes on, and so on. Everyone needs to know these things, no matter what. In personal finance, the comparable skills for this first level are budgeting and debt management.

Drivers at the second level who like to get under the hood a little bit might learn to check the fluid levels and change the oil. Casual drivers might leave such tasks to others, but enthusiastic drivers might do them personally. The driver who is moving to Alaska needs to know how to drive in snow; the driver moving from the United States to England needs to focus on driving on the other side of the road. These are more-specialized skills that not everyone needs to know. For the do-it-yourself individual in personal finance at this second level, we can teach the power of compounding, dollar cost averaging, and diversification.

At the third level, only professional car mechanics should change brake pads and only professional drivers should try to perform at Formula One speeds. In fact, the roads would be a lot less safe if everybody were changing their own brake pads or driving like Michael Schumacher. Skills best left to the expert in personal finance include risk management, asset allocation, and security selection.

The analogies between driver education and investor education are pretty straightforward.

We also need to look at the format and delivery of investor education. The U.S. SEC has a website on how to avoid investment fraud. It is nicely laid out, with the SEC logo in the upper left-hand corner, and the content is strong and very good. If you follow the SEC's advice, you are going to be better off than if you had not done so. It is unclear how engaging it is for users. Another promising format is a YouTube video produced by CFA Institute, "Avoiding Investment Fraud." We need to provide investors with information in a format and place they are expecting and likely to receive it.

We also need to reach investors at the most relevant moment for them. For example, some of the most popular content on the CFA Institute website, which has been picked up by the media and others, is titled "The Top 10 Investment Tips from Rock and Roll." It simply takes lines from songs by such classic bands as the Eagles or the Beatles and infers some fundamental investment truth from them. People love it. I do not know how useful it is in terms of affecting ultimate investment behavior and imparting knowledge, but we do know what it takes to capture people's attention—the first step in any educational process.

Numeracy. Investment education without numeracy is like composition without grammar. You can do it, but you will end up with e-mails that appear to have been written by a teenager.

An interesting study examined the impact of mathematics education on gambling behavior.[3] Not surprisingly, educating people about the mathematics of gambling improves their gambling skill; in particular, they become increasingly resistant to gambling fallacies, such as strings of luck and identifying purported patterns in random data. Interestingly, however, they do not spend any more time or money gambling when they become more educated about the activity.

As a result, investor education must start before people are investors—in fact, before they are savers. Economic literacy in the United States, compared with the rest of the world, is fairly mediocre. According to Tullio Jappelli, we are in the second quartile (where the first quartile is the top), but we are in the low part of that second quartile.[4] This fact is fascinating because we are the world's capitalists. Americans know how markets work. Americans tend to have an intuitive grasp of what it takes to make a market function well. What Americans lack, by and large, is a numerical facility with which to perform analysis. Numeracy is a necessary pre-condition to effective financial literacy.

In addition, numeracy is needed to make sure that we do not create a substitution effect between government intervention and individual responsibility. Jappelli found that, internationally, higher social security contribution rates are

---

[3]Robert J. Williams and Dennis Connolly, "Does Learning about the Mathematics of Gambling Change Gambling Behavior?" *Psychology of Addictive Behaviors,* vol. 20, no. 1 (2006):62–68.
[4]Tullio Jappelli, "Economic Literacy: An International Comparison," *Economic Journal*, vol. 120, no. 548 (November 2010):F429–F451.

actually associated with lower economic literacy. The implication is that those with an incentive to learn tend to do so, and numeracy helps investors respond to that incentive.

Numeracy has also been found to positively affect financial trajectories and outcomes.[5] It is strongly related to wealth levels and changes in wealth. It has an impact on who makes the financial decisions in a household and provides a means of positive interaction for spouses.

Financial Advice. Returning to those three levels of investor skill or interest, it is clear that at some point, people need to leave decision making up to an adviser. So, we need to get people to the right place to obtain advice.

The propensity to seek financial advice depends on people's education level, on their financial literacy, and on their income and wealth (because they have to be able to afford the advice). It also, however, depends on people's experiences. For example, if they experienced a significant drop in income because of bad investment results when investing on their own, they are more likely to seek help.

That investment help or education must make people aware of conflicts of interest in the investment profession, including among their advisers. What does fiduciary duty really mean, and what can they expect of their particular adviser? What is the training and background of that financial intermediary or adviser, and what do his or her credentials mean?

We need to send a simple message and follow the strategy of giving individuals a fishing pole rather than giving them a fish—that is, we should give people the tools to make informed decisions and tell them where to get help about an array of informed decisions rather than telling them what to do in each particular circumstance.

Finally, optimal investment behavior is obviously limited and governed by people's behavioral biases: flaws in our financial memory, the recency effect, hindsight/attribution bias, confirmation bias, and overconfidence. Professionals, including CFA charterholders, are every bit as susceptible to these behavioral biases and cognitive flaws as are nonprofessionals.[6]

---

[5]James Banks, Cormac O'Dea, and Zoë Oldfield, "Cognitive Function, Numeracy and Retirement Saving Trajectories," *Economic Journal*, vol. 120, no. 548 (November 2010):F381–F410.
[6]Stanley B. Block, "A Study of Financial Analysts: Practice and Theory," *Financial Analysts Journal*, vol. 55, no. 4 (July/August 1999):86–95; Michael J. Roszkowski and Glenn E. Snelbecker, "Effects of 'Framing' on Measures of Risk Tolerance: Financial Planners Are Not Immune," *Journal of Behavioral Economics*, vol. 19, no. 3 (Autumn 1990):237–246; Gustaf Torngren and Henry Montgomery, "Worse than Chance? Performance and Confidence among Professionals and Laypeople in the Stock Market," *Journal of Behavioral Finance*, vol. 5, no. 3 (2004):148–153.

What We Can Do. As a profession, we should promote numeracy and economic literacy because these basics constitute the foundation for informed choices and outcomes. We need to keep education simple and focus on the blocking and tackling, the basic concepts. Among these concepts are

- compounding,
- what a safe investment really is (not necessarily a T-bill),
- what diversification actually does and does not do, and
- dollar cost averaging.

We need to remind folks that investing is a complex field; we want to avoid giving the impression that they have knowledge and skills for advanced decision making. Then, we need to educate them about the need for advisement, educate them to become good financial advice consumers by understanding

- the scope of services,
- conflicts of interest, and
- the education and training of various types of advisers.

We also need to educate the advisers. As a representative of CFA Institute, I feel strongly that we should be promoting ethical standards and professional standards among the investment community. We should be educating the investment community about its own behavioral biases.

Finally, we should promote simple controls on investment behavior. Some simple tools will go a long way to help improve investment behavior—for example, an investment diary. In an investment diary, you write down every single investment decision you make: what the decision was and why you made it (for example, buying gold because you think there is going to be hyperinflation in the future). You also document in the diary what the risks to that investment are. If you have ever kept an investment diary and then gone back and revisited that diary a year later, you will have had a very humbling experience because the diary lays bare your own faulty recollection of how good and how reliable your decisions are. Keeping a diary will make you less selective in terms of how you recall your investment performance.

In addition, we can promote the use of investment policy statements and spending diaries.[7] If we promote these simple things, we will end up with more informed investors and better investment decision making.

---

[7]Megan Oaten and Ken Cheng, "Improvements in Self-Control from Financial Monitoring," *Journal of Economic Psychology*, vol. 28, no. 4 (August 2007):487–501.

John Gannon

My focus will be investment fraud—specifically, fraud prevention. It is usually an overlooked area of investor education and financial education. Most people focus on encouraging people to save and reduce debt, but think about it: Even if we are successful in getting people to reduce debt, to save, to have emergency savings accounts and significant nest eggs in their retirement accounts, what happens if even a single corrupt individual gets into somebody's life through, for example, a free investment seminar and, in a short time, is able to take all that money? Traditional financial education does not help consumers or investors address this problem—that is, how to protect themselves from that individual who is going to steal their money.

Most people have heard the adage "If it's too good to be true, it probably isn't true." It contains good advice; the trick is to figure out when "good" is "too good." How are consumers to know—especially when they may be dealing with a fraud expert, someone who is a con artist whose job is to make sure that consumers think whatever he is saying or touting is good and true? That is his job, and he would not be in that job if he were not successful, at least with some individuals, in convincing people that thin air is good and true.

How does he do it, and whom does he target?

The Problem. Fraud is a significant problem in the United States (and around the world, for that matter). Financial fraud has a number of different effects, but we do not even know the full scope of financial fraud because it is hugely underreported. The FINRA Investor Education Foundation did a survey of victims in the United States and found that 78% of those victims did not report to a single person or regulator that they had been defrauded. So, we do not even know the scope of the problem today.

The FINRA Foundation research on financial fraud is trying to (1) identify the victims of the fraud (specifically, investment fraud), (2) understand what tactics are being used against those individuals, and then (3) develop preventative steps to protect investors.

The Victims. One of the first questions the FINRA Foundation asked is, Who is the likely victim of investment fraud? The answer may surprise you: a male, 55–65 years of age, married, more financially literate, college educated, recently subjected to a change in financial or health status, a risk taker, self-directed, and overly optimistic. Keep in mind that, although the target audience is 55–65 years of age, that finding does not mean that such people are the most *susceptible* to investment fraud. But typically, such people have the net worth to make investments. They *are* making investments. Younger people actually may be more susceptible to investment fraud but simply do not have the assets to become a focused target of fraudsters.

The fact that the likely victim is financially literate is used by some people as an indication that financial literacy does not help. I would argue that *traditional* financial literacy is irrelevant to protecting people from investment fraud or financial fraud because what financial fraud is all about is getting people to make an emotional rather than a logical decision.

Consider the example of Bernie Madoff. Madoff fooled some very, very sophisticated investors—institutional investors. How did he do that? Those victims were smart people, extremely financially literate, and sophisticated. He did it through emotion and psychology.

So, the FINRA Foundation decided to examine what kinds of risky behavior people engage in that opens them to victimhood. If you walk into a room of investors, most of them will deny that they are susceptible to investment fraud. If you look at the victims versus nonvictims, you find the true differences: The victims engage in certain activities that make them vulnerable to risk and fraud. For example, 73% of victims, but only 58% of the foundation's national sample of investors, have owned such risky investments as hedge funds or penny stocks; 70% of victims, but only a third of the national sample, have made an investment based solely on the advice of a friend, a family member, or coworker. Three times as many victims as nonvictims attended a free lunch investment seminar. The victims are more open to the con artist's appeal.

Consider another result. We at the FINRA Foundation sent the survey out to victims and nonvictims. The result was that 50% of the victims responded to our survey, whereas only 10% of the general investing population did. Even getting something in the mail is an enticement for victims to respond.

The Tactics. The next thing the FINRA Foundation looked at was what tactics fraudsters use. In looking at all types of financial fraud, the foundation discovered, first, that with respect to investment fraud, twice as many psychological tactics were used than in other types of financial fraud, such as lottery fraud. We identified specifically what those tactics were by looking at fraud tapes (tapes made by law enforcement agents posing as investors) of pitched calls from fraudsters. The researchers catalogued the various tactics and identified which tactics were the most used. They found the most common tactics in investment fraud to be the lure of phantom riches, source credibility, social consensus, reciprocity, and scarcity.

- *Phantom riches.* This tactic tempts someone with the promise of wealth or a high or guaranteed return.

- *Source credibility.* Credibility is easy to fake. For example, why am I wearing a suit and a nice tie today? I am doing it to appear credible. If you do not know who I am, I can fake credibility. I can put a diploma on my wall from Harvard University that could be totally fake.

- *Social consensus.* If everybody is doing it, it must be right. This reasoning is a shortcut we all take. We look around at our friends and coworkers, and if they are participating in an investment, we think we can short-circuit our own due diligence and invest. The appeal to social consensus is one of Madoff's tricks: "Everybody in the synagogue is doing it; everybody at the country club is doing it. So, it has to be okay, right?" It works.

- *Reciprocity.* If somebody gives you a small gift, you feel you owe them a gift in return. This tactic lies behind the free investment seminar. Somebody buys you a $10 chicken dinner, and what does he expect back? A gift. This approach works well. Social researchers have done a number of tests on it.[8] One researcher sent 100 holiday cards to the first 100 people in the phone book. How many responses did he get to those holiday cards? These are people he did not even know, and yet he got 50 cards back. Here is another example. We have all received those little sticky address labels in the mail from a charity. Did you know that this little gift doubles the response rate to that charity? That is why they send those labels to you. It is reciprocity at work.

- *Scarcity.* This approach is what we call the "closing" tactic. The verbiage is something like "Only a limited number of shares are left!" or "This is a limited-time offer." The fraudster has been wrapping you in emotion, right? She has used the previous tactics and hot buttons. She has tried to get to know you. Now, to close the deal before you get out, she uses scarcity as an additional hot button.

Investment fraud is psychological, so teaching people about diversification of risk has nothing to do with combating it. Con artists are not trying to induce you to make a rational, logical decision with respect to investments. They are trying to overwhelm you by using psychological tactics so that you do not think, which is how Madoff was able to con smart, sophisticated investors. Those people were not thinking with their heads. They were thinking with their hearts.

Outsmarting Investment Fraud. What FINRA is trying to do—and it may be unique among securities regulators—is to move beyond what most people in the regulatory world, even the financial education field, do, to go beyond warning campaigns about fraud. In a warning campaign, we issue an investor alert about a scam we see. The problem with that approach is, first,

---

[8] *The Psychology of Scams: Provoking and Committing Errors of Judgement* (U.K. Office of Fair Trading, 2009); "Off the Hook Again," Consumer Fraud Research Group (2006); "Examining Consumer Policy: A Report on Consumer Information Campaigns Concerning Scams," Organisation for Economic Co-Operation and Development (December 2005); "Off the Hook: Reducing Participation in Telemarketing Fraud," AARP (2003); Jonathan J. Rusch, "The 'Social Engineering' of Internet Fraud," U.S. Department of Justice (1999): http://www.isoc.org/inet99/proceedings/3g/3g_2.htm.

we're warning about a specific scam that is already in existence. So, investors have probably already been harmed. It is a reactive strategy. We issue that alert, warn people about the scam, issue a press release, and that is about it. We inform people, "Here is the scam; here is how it works; do not fall for it." Boom, done. We stir up a lot of interest for a short period of time.

We are trying to improve on that strategy by educating people about financial fraud in general. It is not tailored to a specific type of scam. We make the information *generic*; we develop a program that applies to all types of fraud. We want the consumer to be able to use the information regardless of what type of investment fraud is being perpetrated. The strategy is *proactive*, and it is a *long-term effort* in which we continue to help people understand the educational message.

Finally, the proactive strategy is *skills based*, not reliant on issuing information. We teach people skills they can use to protect themselves from investment fraud. We have developed a three-part curriculum.

1. We start with teaching people about the risk of fraud because if you ask a room of investors about fraud, the first thing each one will say is, "It's not me who's at risk; it's the other guy." We make sure that they understand that they *are* at risk of investment fraud.

2. We teach them to recognize the persuasion tactics that I have described. That is all we teach them—the *tactics*, not the specifics of a particular fraud, not what a Ponzi scheme, pump and dump, or any other specific scheme is. We teach them the persuasion tactics because those tactics underlie every type of fraud.

3. We teach two simple but powerful prevention steps. First, ask a lot of questions. Questions typically throw a fraudster off his game. Second, verify the information. Specifically, verify that the person persuading you is licensed to sell an investment product and that the product is registered. Are these steps going to avoid all types of investment fraud? Absolutely not. Will they avoid the worst types? I believe so.

We tested the curriculum we developed in two field experiments—one in 2008 and one in 2009. In 2008, we recruited groups to go through workshops; we delivered the new curriculum to the first group and designated the other group—the control group—not to have the new presentation. Then, three and a half days after they had been through the program, we had a telemarketer pitch everybody on a fake oil and gas scam.

What we saw was a measurable difference in resistance to fraud appeal between the people who had received the new curriculum and those who had not. Only about 18% of the group that had been through the experiment responded to the pitch by giving personal identifying information so they could receive more information, but 36% of the uninstructed group succumbed to the pitch—a 50% difference. That result was good. Then, we repeated the experiment in 2009. We wanted to confirm the results of the experiment, and we wanted to test persistence, which means that instead of hitting people with the telemarketer pitch only three days after the presentation, we hit people two and a half weeks later. We had the same results.

So, the curriculum works. But how should one deliver it? We have worked tremendously to make sure it is available to anyone—particularly, any regulator or nonprofit—in any form desired. The formats include a documentary (on the model of Al Gore's *An Inconvenient Truth*) that is titled "Tricks of the Trade: Outsmarting Investment Fraud." It is available for free on DVD. We have distributed 30,000 copies on DVD, but more importantly, we were able to get WQED, a Pittsburgh PBS station, to sponsor it for us, and it is now on PBS. In our first year of showing it on PBS, we had more than 50 million house-holds see the documentary, which is a significant reach for a program. We also provide tool kits, flip charts, and handouts (even in the form of playing cards). We work with many partners, including AARP and state security regulators, to distribute the materials.

The FINRA Foundation continues to work on the project to stamp out investment fraud. We are now working with the Stanford Center on Longevity, and we have set up a research center to explore more areas of research. We are using FMRI (functional magnetic resonance imaging) technology to examine investors broadly construed and the subset consisting of known victims of investment fraud. The search is to answer two questions: (1) Are known victims of investment fraud more influenced by these persuasion tactics? (2) Are victims of investment fraud less able to learn from their mistakes? In other words, are people who became victims less able to learn from previous losses? If so, that area may be one in which we can educate people further.

Peter Tufano

Americans have a massive knowledge deficit with respect to their finances. Annamaria Lusardi has done a lot of work on this topic, a bit with me. For example, we did a study on debt literacy—defined as people's ability to make very simple decisions about debt—to understand the financial implications of borrowing on a credit card.[9] We found that only about a third of people can answer correctly questions about how interest compounds. We found that men, by and large, do considerably better than women, that very young adults (younger than 30 years of age) perform less well than middle-age people, that wealthy people do better than poor people, and that senior citizens do particularly poorly.

---

[9]Annamaria Lusardi and Peter Tufano, "Debt Literacy, Financial Experiences, and Overindebtedness," NBER Working Paper No. 14808 (March 2009).

On that last point I want to emphasize one thing. Part of our research consisted of a battery of questions to find out whether people understood basic concepts of finance. We also asked them to rate themselves in terms of their knowledge of finance. One group stood out: senior citizens. They had the lowest knowledge on objective questions but the highest scores for judging themselves to be knowledgeable. This dissonance between perceived knowledge and actual skills is massive and contributes to their heightened susceptibility to investment fraud. It is particularly a problem because we ask senior citizens to make one of the most complex decisions of their life—which is the spend-down or draw-down from their retirement plans—at a time when their overall cognitive abilities are being challenged.

Does this knowledge deficit among Americans matter? In the work on debt literacy, Anna and I found, after controlling for age, wealth, income, education, and all the other factors that might influence the financial choices made by individuals, that people who were less knowledgeable about debt tended to use higher-cost borrowing methods and to judge themselves to be overindebted. Can I, as an economist, say that there is a causal link between those two findings? No, but it is striking that the people who knew the least on our tests were the people who transacted in the most disadvantaged way and ended up quite unprepared to deal with the implications and levels of the debt they had taken on. They judged themselves to be overindebted.

The Information Problem. We might hope that financial institutions can solve these problems for us. Unfortunately, these results are not encouraging either. For example, in a paper I co-authored a few years ago, we examined the investment performance of broker-sold funds.[10] We found that before deducting a single penny for the marketing costs of these funds, the alpha the funds delivered was considerably worse than the alpha before marketing costs for directly sold funds. Furthermore, when we examined the aggregate to see whether fund managers had any ability to time the market, we saw none. We scratched our heads and hoped we could find some other benefit that the adviser community had been delivering because it certainly was not delivering performance, even before deducting any fees for marketing. No benefits were captured by the tangible measures we explored.

---

[10]Daniel B. Bergstresser, John Chalmers, and Peter Tufano, "Assessing the Costs and Benefits of Brokers in the Mutual Fund Industry," *Review of Financial Studies*, vol. 22, no. 10 (October 2009):4129–4156.

Consider also research on the banking industry. I wrote a case study about a bank that had built part of its business model around debit accounts and credit cards.[11] The case revolved around a manager who was trying to determine which accounts the bank should open for customers.

Here is the economics of the bank's business model: About 11% of the people who opened up bank accounts—consisting of debit cards and checking accounts—never overdrew their accounts. They were angels. Another 78% were like you and me; they overdrew once or twice. They went on vacation, they forgot about something, the bill was late in the mail, and they overdrew. Then, another 11% overdrew more than 50 times a year, each time paying a charge of between $25 and $27. These "bad" customers were massively subsidizing the "good" customers.

This business model is common in banks. These banks are not compensating for the knowledge deficit on the part of consumers but, rather, are exploiting it. So, the first priority is to provide consumers with better information than they are getting now. Some of the information that consumers now receive is hard to understand, so providing simpler and easier to understand information is a priority. In a recent paper, my co-authors and I identified information as one of the things that regulators can provide.[12] And although this step may be necessary, it is not sufficient.

The second improvement that can be made is in the architecture for making choices, as best summarized by Thaler and Sunstein in *Nudge*.[13] This line of work is changing how default choices are made, particularly in the pension world, where it has proven to be extraordinarily successful. For example, the Pension Protection Act makes it easier for pensions to default employees into investing.

Third, we can encourage financial institutions to deliver better products and services and hold them to higher fiduciary duties. My lawyer friends will tell me that imposing fiduciary duties on somebody is just the beginning of a conversation, not the end. In some sense, it requires *ex post* resolution in the courts as opposed to *ex ante* actions. Yet, as a society, we must determine what the "rules of the game" are for firms competing in retail financial services, which do business with some very ill-equipped customers. In the end, however, financial education still has an important role. Consumers must be able to make good decisions. Although defaults are important, we cannot structure all the decisions

---

[11]Dennis Campbell, Francisco de Asis Martinez-Jerez, Peter Tufano, and Emily McClintock, "Central Bank: The ChexSystem Qualifile® Decision," Harvard Business School Case 208-029 (July 2007).

[12]John Campbell, Howell Jackson, Brigitte Madrian, and Peter Tufano, "Consumer Financial Protection," *Journal of Economic Perspectives*, vol. 25, no. 1 (Winter 2011):91–114.

[13]Richard Thaler and Cass R. Sunstein, *Nudge: Improving Decisions about Health, Wealth, and Happiness* (Ann Arbor, MI: Caravan Books, 2008).

consumers must make. We cannot assume that every financial institution that consumers are going to deal with will offer them the absolute best product or the product that is best for them. So, what do we do about financial education?

Improving Information Delivery. We know roughly what consumers need to know, but we do not spend much time on how to deliver that information or on the most effective delivery channels. I will focus my remarks mostly on delivery channels because that is where I think all the action is. I want to make three points, and I will illustrate them with some of the things we have done at the Doorways to Dreams Fund, Harvard, and elsewhere. I will discuss (1) using just-in-time education, (2) making financial education engaging, and (3) making it ubiquitous.

First, just-in-time education kicks in at the point, or just before the point, at which someone is going to make a decision. Educators are big fans of creating comprehensive educational programs, but consumer education needs to identify not only what consumers need to know but also that they need to know it. There are opportunities to create intervention points where people can get the information they want. For example, a "buy versus lease" session in a classroom may be more effective if supplemented by an "app" that a consumer can use in an auto showroom.

Second, and more importantly, we have to accept that all education is voluntary. Even in the military, you can force troops to sit in a room and listen, but you cannot force them to hear. One thing I learned after 22 years at Harvard Business School is that making the material engaging and something people want to learn may not be terribly efficient, but it can be terribly effective. For this reason, at the Doorways to Dreams Fund, we have been working on a concept we call "financial entertainment." It shamelessly aims to be popular. We are creating opportunities for people to learn concepts and have fun simultaneously. The word "fun" is in my vocabulary a lot. We have five entertainment titles so far. The first, a video game, is "Celebrity Calamity," available free on iTunes. The story line is simple. You, the player, are the financial manager of a screwed-up celebrity. You have a debit card and a credit card and a little account, and you have to manage the celebrity's money. Our first instructions to our game developers—and we work with commercial developers—were to make it fun: "We know how to make it boring. It is your job to make it fun." For example, in another game, BiteClub, we "amp up" the consequences of pension investing decisions by taking the perspective of a vampire-investor: When you're immortal, retirement is eternal!

Our approach may not be the only way to solve the lack of consumer education, but we sometimes forget, as we earnestly put forth seminars and workshops, that we have to communicate and reach people one on one, wherever they are. We think financial entertainment is one way to reach out.

Third, financial education needs to be made ubiquitous. In the numerous conferences on financial literacy, the general agreement is that we need to make sure that all young people are taught the financial skills they need. We need to make sure that courses about financial education are in every curriculum.

I have debated with people in secondary and primary education about what should be in the core curriculum. Huge disagreements arise in general about what gets in the curriculum and what does not. Can we fit financial education in there? I would like to make an outrageous suggestion: We hijack not only the SAT exam but also the PSAT and ACT exams. About half of all high school students take these high-stakes exams, which include large sections on math and quantitative reasoning. When I talked to some of the people who design these tests, I found they do not care if the exam tests whether two trains are coming closer together or whether the balances on a savings and an investment account are getting further apart. As long as the exam tests the specified math skills, the designers are indifferent. So, we propose to change the context, but not the content, of the exams; the mathematical and analytical content will be the same. We propose allowing the context for much of the exam to relate to financial questions.

This proposal is important not because the exam itself will make any difference in the world—it lasts only a few hours—*but* if the exam changes, every test preparation organization will follow suit. We have a major test prep organization working with us. It has mocked up what the exam would look like and has given some thought to what its curriculum would look like.

Using the world of personal finance as the context for math in these exams would also send another important signal. Financial education has, up to this point, largely been a remedial subject for bottom-of-the-class students. Students who go to college generally do not take financial education classes. This proposal would turn that paradigm on its head, requiring students who want to go to the top schools in the world, as well as the kids who are never going to go to college, to participate in financial education. It would send a message to parents and educators that, in fact, financial literacy is important for everyone. The marginal cost of making financial education ubiquitous would be close to zero. We can make financial education part of millions of young people's everyday experience.

Chris Farrell

My perspective is shaped by the work I have done in public radio, the radio documentaries I have done, and my time spent in public housing complexes in Chicago and Memphis, Tennessee, finding out about financial literacy there.

I have several key points. First, financial literacy is more important than it used to be. Second, low-income families do not have money to waste. Third, we are asking too much of individuals when it comes to financial literacy, and we are not focusing enough on institutional solutions.

Importance of Financial Literacy Today. Financial literacy matters more than ever before primarily because more people are in 401(k) or 403(b) retirement savings plans; thus, more people have to make decisions about their retirement. But more than just retirement savings plans requires financial literacy; people need to understand 529 college savings plans and manage other assets. We are asking more of ourselves. In addition, the poor no longer move into public housing complexes; they get housing vouchers. They have been moved toward a market system, which is asking a lot more of individuals in terms of requiring them to make decisions.

Public policy for the past 30–40 years has been to democratize credit. Policies enable lower- and middle-income people to get credit that was once available only to the affluent. This policy has a lot of benefits, but the merchants of debt are also quite good at selling the benefits of debt while hiding the real costs.

One part of financial literacy, in particular, has been underestimated. It is the aspect of literacy that enables people to borrow sensibly and to save. People need to know the basics that bring them into the mainstream of society. Addressing these issues is part of the solution to the much bigger issue of alleviating poverty.

When it comes to financial literacy, we have two universes. One universe consists of working-class and middle-class families, who face the kinds of questions that a financial adviser would be great at answering. Most advisers do not want to have anything to do with these families, however, because they cannot make money off them. These families have questions about their 401(k), their 403(b), the 529 college savings plan, the Roth IRA. The questions I get most frequently on Marketplace Money right now are in two areas: (1) student loans and (2) retirement savings.

There is a great deal of confusion about student loans to pay for college as an undergraduate and to pay for graduate school. "What is the difference between a federal student loan and a private student loan?" "How much can I borrow?"

The second set of questions is asked by people around 55–65 years of age. "What's my 'number'?" "Have I saved enough?" "I saved in my 403(b), so how much can I take out each year? No one will tell me."

Money in Low-Income Households. The other universe for financial literacy is low-income families. Being poor is really costly. It costs a lot of money. We saw what happened to lower-income people with the subprime market, but it is not just the subprime market that presents challenges for the poor. Suppose a young woman wants to leave home and move into her own apartment. She decides to rent furniture. How does she figure out what is the real cost of that rental furniture? A young man can buy a used car with no credit check, but what is the real price of that car? What is the price of the payday loan? Knowing the answers to these questions is a different form of financial literacy from the savings questions, and the market is different from the one we are accustomed to dealing with, but this kind of financial literacy is extremely important.

How are we doing with educating the public about financial matters? The financial profession is doing well in terms of financial literacy in some areas. Gains have been made, particularly among middle-income households. When I started taking personal finance questions in public radio in the 1980s, most of the questions were about certificates of deposit (CDs). That was it. Everyone wanted to know how to find a high-yielding CD. Fischer Black gave a wonderful American Finance Association presidential address in 1985 called "Noise," in which he talked about all the noise out there.[14] As well as information and knowledge, we have gossip and rumors, which is why we operate with rules of thumb. The rules of thumb have become more sophisticated over time among a certain group of people. Now, in public radio, we talk about risk and return, about asset allocation, and about diversification.

In the poor neighborhoods, however, you will see the popularity, even now, of payday lending, of renting furniture. Not a lot of progress has been made in that part of the market.

Need for Institutional Support. When it comes to financial literacy, we are simply asking too much of individuals. Think about a two-income couple with children in 1968 versus now. The couple today is working 20% more hours than the couple in 1968. Employers demand a lot of people's time. Moreover, work is not our only activity. My late dad used to travel a lot, and when he came home, we had dinner and then my parents would have a Scotch and watch Walter Cronkite, and we would go off and do our homework. Today, a father or mother does homework with the kids. People want to be healthy, so we have to decide carefully what to eat and then we have to exercise. In addition, we want to volunteer in our community. The result is that the amount of effort involved in what is considered a full life has really increased. The literacy that people are supposed to have about exercise, about diet, and about their jobs has gone up correspondingly. And now, on top of all this, they are supposed to be financially literate. People are expected to be Wall Street brokers—or better yet, be able to outwit one. We are asking an awful lot of ourselves, so institutional support and institutional reform really matter.

Thomas Kane, the wonderful education economist, told the following story. He was working for Joseph Stiglitz, who was chairman of the Council of Economic Advisers. One day, Kane saw a frustrated Stiglitz at a conference table, with papers strewn all over the place. Kane thought, "Oh, boy, is the President upset? What is going on here?" It turned out that Stiglitz was

---

[14]Fischer Black, "Noise," *Journal of Finance*, vol. 41, no. 3 (July 1986):529–543.

filling out the Free Application for Federal Student Aid (FAFSA) for one of his children. It is, indeed, a difficult form to complete. Stiglitz, one of the most brilliant men in the world, found that out. Parents with a lot less brain power, including me, have found it out also.

A wonderful study by Bettinger, Long, Oreopoulos, and Sanbonmatsu argues that FAFSA is a barrier for low-income families who might apply for college.[15] In the study, the control group received good information for filling out the forms. They spent time on the internet and put effort into the task. The other group, in addition to the information, worked with professionals at H&R Block. They had someone to talk to, someone to translate the information for them. The students who worked with the professionals were 40% more likely to apply for financial aid than the well-informed control group. This improvement came simply from offering support.

One story I reported on for American RadioWorks, the public documentary unit, came from the public housing projects in Memphis. A foundation, the city government, and some banks are conducting a project with individual development accounts (IDAs). To qualify for the matching funds in an IDA, a person has to participate in a financial literacy program. The person also must have a goal—own a home, get a college education, start a business—and then can receive a matching grant. In Memphis, for every dollar that a person saves, $2 goes into that person's account.

We talked to a 34-year-old secretary working at a junior high school who had four children and who had been participating in this program for a year and a half. When we met her, she had just bought her home, and she and her kids had moved out of the public housing complex. The house payment was actually less than what she had been paying in rent. She then opened up savings accounts for all of her kids, and she still has her home. She received institutional support. A study by the Urban Institute has found that for people who go through this type of program, where they get not only financial literacy but also institutional support from an IDA program, the foreclosure rate is 30–50% lower than for those who do not.[16]

---

[15]Eric P. Bettinger, Bridget Terry Long, Philip Oreopoulos, and Lisa Sanbonmatsu, "The Role of Simplification and Information in College Decisions: Results from the H&R Block FAFSA Experiment," NBER Working Paper No. 15361 (June 2010): https://cepa.stanford.edu/sites/default/files/Bettinger%20Long%20Oreopoulos%20Sanbonmatsu%20-%20FAFSA%20paper%201-22-12.pdf.

[16]Ida Rademacher, Kasey Wiedrich, Signe-Mary McKernan, Caroline Ratcliffe, and Megan Gallagher, "Weathering the Storm: Have IDAs Helped Low-Income Homebuyers Avoid Foreclosure?" Urban Institute and CFED (April 2010): http://www.urban.org/UploadedPDF/412064_weathering_the_storm.pdf.

Many people are dealing with the move toward 401(k) plans instead of defined-benefit pension plans. They show up at work and indicate how much they want in stocks, how much in bonds, and so on. They are making such decisions, but an enormous amount of evidence from behavioral economics and behavioral finance indicates that most people, even the people in this room, are pretty poor at investing. I think we need to remove decisions from, not add decisions to, the burden of the individual.

A great savings program, although it is having some trouble right now, is Social Security. A contribution is simply taken out of your paycheck; then, when you retire, a defined payment is available. A number of researchers advocated putting voluntary individual retirement accounts on top of Social Security—very simple, very limited in terms of the number of investment choices. Nobel Laureate Robert Fogel has gone further with these ideas by suggesting what is, I think, the most intriguing idea of all: mandatory savings. Such money would go into a program resembling TIAA-CREF or federal thrift programs. The program would offer very limited choices, be very broad-based, and have very low fees. Mandatory savings—no fuss, no muss. You get to be 55 or 60, and you know you have some money in your plan. These types of plans remove a lot of decision making from people, thus freeing them up to expend energy on other things, such as creating new businesses.

Other ideas pertain to making saving as easy as borrowing. We make borrowing really easy; we should make saving equally easy. Roy Sutherland, an advertising executive at Ogilvy & Mather, suggested a couple of years ago that if every checkout clerk had to say, "Would you like to add to your savings today?" people would save more. Not a bad idea. He wanted a big red button in everyone's living room that, every time someone hit it, $50 would go into that person's savings account. It sounds funny, but today, some applications are being created for the iPhone and Android that ask you whether you want to put into your savings the amount you saved because something was on sale. Technology may open up some avenues for impulse saving, not just impulse buying.

To conclude, we have created a system in which lots of people have to make financial choices that they really do not want to be making and are not equipped to make. A lot of people are not very good at making financial choices—among them are college professors and radio professionals, highly educated people who are not good at making long-term money decisions. Financial literacy is good, absolutely. It is important. But I think what is more important is institutional reforms that help people make better choices.

Question and Answer Session

Question: Professor Tufano, I was listening particularly closely when you were talking about your friends from financial institutions suggesting that the call for better fiduciary responsibility is the beginning, not the end, of the inquiry. When I hear that statement in the context of my advocacy in Washington for the authentic fiduciary standard, a red flag goes up. The flag goes up because some of the industry friends that we have in common are suggesting that we should slow way down and be very careful in terms of applying this standard. Therefore, I think what you've suggested could be heard as suggesting that we should not apply the standard to everyone who delivers investment advice. Could you extend your remarks on that point?

Tufano: I'm not a lawyer, but as a trustee of mutual fund complexes and as a researcher, I spend some time thinking about fiduciary duties. One should not interpret my comments as suggesting that the standards of fiduciary duty should be lowered; rather, I suspect that they should be higher and more broadly adopted. There is the carrot approach, the stick approach, and the common standards approach. We can reward great firms, punish poorly performing ones, or try to get everyone to meet minimal standards. We need to consider all three approaches, but we should certainly not lower standards of fiduciary behavior.

Horan: The points about fiduciary care have great relevance for CFA Institute and CFA charterholders. The duty of care by which our members are bound is one we would certainly describe (taking into account differences in the use of this word among countries) as *fiduciary*. We need to think about when that duty can be imposed and when it cannot. In a good many situations, it cannot. For example, I don't expect a level of fiduciary care from my used car salesman. I'm not looking to him for advice. I'm looking to him for car information and to present me with products.

A broker selling an IPO to an investor cannot possibly be a fiduciary because a fiduciary must place the client's interest first, foremost, and exclusively above his or her own and anyone else's. By definition, if you are acting as a broker, you have an interest on the other side of the trade. We do not permit attorneys to represent both sides of a lawsuit. They cannot be fiduciaries in that way. I think we need to be thoughtful about where and when that standard can be applied.

Question: No one explicitly said that there should be reasonable default investment decisions for customers who do not explicitly make any decisions themselves. Shouldn't more effort go into designing good default decisions?

Horan: Default selections, I would argue, do not constitute education. Default choices are a substitute for education. Our notion of when to impose defaults should be informed by what we can expect from our educational efforts. With regard to the efficacy of the efforts to design good programs with default decisions, the evidence is not favorable, with the exception of some innovative programs that Peter Tufano has outlined. Programs where the format, delivery, and style speak to the learner are a lot more effective.

Farrell: Having good default choices is extremely important but hard to do—an example being the target date fund. The original idea about making the target date fund a default choice was good. As it has evolved, however, it has become problematic. Target date funds may hold junk bonds and other kinds of weird stuff that I don't think was part of the original idea behind having a good default fund. More effort needs to be put into default choices.

Question: Some of the Society of Actuaries' research points out that housing is 70% of the assets of middle-income people who are 55–74 years old. Financial advisers, as you pointed out, aren't very interested in this group, so I believe we need to improve the software used by this segment. The Society of Actuaries' studies of software and postretirement decisions found that the software either doesn't focus well on the key issues or it handles them wrongly. What does the panel think of the software? And in connection with the importance of advisers, how should one deliver advice, particularly to lower-income people who are not going to pay for the advice?

Gannon: When FINRA started developing tools for its website, I was astonished that when I went to buy data feeds and get consultants to work on these projects, *data integrity* was a big issue. I thought we would need to focus on getting the lowest cost providers, but we had to focus on data integrity. A lot of data feeds that we take for granted, that underlie many of our software tools, are highly inaccurate. The math underlying many of these tools is also inaccurate. We have hired and retained an auditor to verify the math behind all of our tools. He has also double-checked the tools of other organizations. It's a serious issue because many people are not making the effort to ensure that their data are accurate.

Farrell: Some improvement has been made with the software. If you go back 20 years, filling out Microsoft Money or Quicken took a lot of dedication. Now, programs like mint.com have made it a lot easier to graph your debt and graph your spending. My bank is now offering a version of mint.com. I believe the software is going to improve further.

Question: Electronic presentations that teach people about money in a fun and entertaining way are fun to make, but is there any evidence that they are effective?

Tufano: Our particular work on using entertainment as an effective method of education is exploratory at best. The best evidence I've seen is not in the area of financial education but in health education. For a program called "Re-Mission" (a space invaders game), which was done by HopeLabs, a randomized control trial showed that the use of the program by kids with cancer improves their compliance with taking their medications. In addition, some other studies suggest that popular culture can modify behavior—at least that is the hypothesis under which we are working.

Gannon: Although there isn't much evidence out there for the effectiveness of TV and other media, Robert Cialdini, a psychologist at Arizona State University, has conducted some experiments with TV and split cable (so that you can test a control group against an experimental group that receives education or advice via TV and see if the latter group does better).

Question: The group for which personal bankruptcy is growing fastest is college students. They're graduating with more than $20,000 in debt, and at the same time, the credit card issuers are pursuing them aggressively. There is a real need for college-educated people to have this information because they're blowing up right at the time when they otherwise might be buying a home. What programs are being dedicated to this group?

Gannon: I appreciated Chris Farrell's comments because I think simple techniques can be used to improve the decisions that college students are making. FINRA is about to release a paper that was written for us by the Institute for College Access and Success, which looks at the counseling provided to recipients of private versus federally guaranteed student loans. The number one form of consumer debt in this country now is student loans. A lot of work can easily be done in this area.

Question: Mr. Farrell, you said that one of the goals of financial education is to bring low-income people into the mainstream of society. However, it seems as though we're getting more information to the middle class but not to lower-income people. For example, if financial literacy is used in the SAT, the effect will be to make those who are already fairly well off in society even more so, rather than to target actual low-income people. What progress is being made toward that goal of bringing financial literacy to lower-income people?

Farrell: It is always bad to be poor, but soon, it is going to be worse than usual. At the state, local, and federal levels, the spending cuts are being targeted at the poor. The kinds of IDAs that Peter Tufano described for promoting savings and other efforts intended to help the poor are extremely important. There is evidence that they do help, but if tax money is involved, there will be a lot of pullback.

Tufano: Most of the work that I do deals with low- to moderate-income families. Having said that, I'd like to recognize that the debt loads of college students are quite high. Delivering financial literacy for college students who may end up with massive student loan debt, at zero cost or near-zero cost, addresses a real financial need.

Session 2: Housing Decisions: Do Consumers Know What They Need to Know?

Disclosure in the Mortgage Market

Paul Willen
Senior Economist and Policy Advisor
Federal Reserve Bank of Boston

This presentation is based on a paper in progress with Kris Gerardi and Andreas Fuster titled "Information and Borrower Choice Behavior in the Mortgage Market." I will focus more narrowly today on the Consumer Financial Protection Bureau's (CFPB's) proposed disclosure to borrowers who are getting a mortgage.[1]

Consumer Disclosure Requirements for Mortgages

The idea behind the CFPB's disclosure is that borrowers need a simple, clear explanation of the important parts of their mortgage. They are not going to read through 100 pages of disclosure; they are not going to read the contract itself; they are not going to read the riders of the contract. But they need to know key pieces of information.

At the top of the proposed form are the key loan terms, which show the interest rate and how it could change, the monthly payment and how it could change, and the taxes and insurance and how they could change.

The next area contains cautions: Is there a possibility of a balloon payment? Is there a possibility of a prepayment penalty, and can the loan balance increase? At the bottom of the form is a description of how the payment will evolve over the life of the mortgage. And just above that is a calculation of how the principal balance will change in five years, or how much of the mortgage will have been paid off in five years.

Reviewing the form, one sees that the CFPB devoted much of the prime real estate on it to conveying information about how payments change over time. The motivation for this choice is, of course, the accepted wisdom that the foreclosure crisis resulted from the fact that many borrowers did not realize

---

[1]See www.consumerfinance.gov/knowbeforeyouowe/compare/ to view the proposed disclosure forms.

that their payments would rise and thus lost their homes when they could not afford the higher payments. But this is a misconception. As I will show later, payment shocks accounted for a very small fraction of the foreclosures in the crisis. Instead, as we have argued over and over again, the main driver of foreclosures was falling house prices.

In what follows, I first show the evidence that payment changes did not cause the vast majority of foreclosures, devoting particular attention to option ARMs (adjustable-rate mortgages), without a doubt the most confusing products and the ones, in theory, that made borrowers most vulnerable to payment shocks. I then review the evidence on the role of falling house prices in causing foreclosures.

I conclude by discussing what I think a good disclosure form needs to do. Broadly speaking, the goal of disclosure is to prevent households from making bad decisions, but the problem is that the millions of Americans who buy homes all need to know different things to avoid making a mistake. In my opinion, comparatively few people made bad decisions because they didn't understand payment changes, so it makes little sense to devote most of the form to payment changes. In contrast, I think many Americans made bad decisions because they didn't appreciate just how volatile house prices could be, and I propose that the most valuable information the CFPB can provide is about house prices.

Payment Changes and Mortgage Defaults

To many in policy circles, the long-term fully amortizing, fixed-rate mortgage (FRM) is an inherently safe product, and it was our repudiation of them in favor of ARMs during the mid-2000s that led to the crisis. According to this view, payment shocks are the main reason why borrowers default, and by eliminating payment shocks, the FRM eliminates most risk from a mortgage.

Early in the crisis, we learned that this view was wrong. In the first part of 2007, we examined the data for borrowers in Massachusetts who were defaulting on adjustable-rate mortgages, and we found that almost all of them were having payment problems long before the payment on the mortgage changed. The payment shock, a surprise increase in the payment, could not be driving the defaults we saw.

Over the years, we have gone from having a sample of hundreds of loans in Massachusetts to national samples containing millions of loans, but the story remains the same. **Table 1** shows tabulations based on a sample of loans for which the lender initiated foreclosure proceedings. To measure the role of payment shocks, we went back to the month when the borrower first missed a payment in the delinquency spell that led to the foreclosure. We then checked to see if the payment due that month was different from the initial payment (when the borrower first got the mortgage).

Table 1. Payment Changes and Default

	2007	2008	2009	2010	All
FRM share	38%	48%	62%	74%	59%
Prior to delinquency spell that led to foreclosure, percentage of loans with . . .					
Reset	18%	20%	18%	11%	17%
Payment increase	12	17	11	9	12
Payment reduction	0	0	4	8	4
No change since origination	88	82	85	83	84
Private label	68%	54%	37%	23%	41%
Number of observations (thousands)	374	641	874	756	2,646

We found, for the four years of the crisis, that only 12% of borrowers were making a higher payment at the time they became delinquent on their loan than they were when they got the loan. The main reason for that finding is that nearly 60% of the loans on which foreclosure proceedings had been initiated were fixed-rate mortgages, which cannot have a payment change. Another big chunk of these mortgages were adjustable-rate mortgages. But because interest rates were so low, they actually reset to the same or a lower number when the payments changed.

In other words, one cannot attribute the vast majority of the foreclosures in the crisis to payment shocks in adjustable-rate mortgages. If we had converted all the adjustable-rate mortgages to fixed mortgages, that would have affected payments for only 12% of the troubled borrowers. Even for those 12%, it is not clear that eliminating the payment shock would have prevented foreclosure because, as the table illustrates, millions of borrowers ended up in foreclosure without payment shocks!

Option ARMs

No discussion of payment shocks is complete without a discussion of the option ARM. Perhaps many ARMs were innocuous and did not play a role in the crisis, but the option ARM is the poster child for a predatory product. A *Businessweek* article from 10 September 2006 said, "The option adjustable-rate mortgage, the option ARM, might be the riskiest and most complicated home loan product ever created."[2] And this is one of the less nasty quotes.

Option ARMs are incredibly confusing, and indeed as researchers, our first reaction was that they were designed for no other purpose than to confuse consumers. But as we spent time learning about the option ARM, we saw that it is actually a very logical, sensible product—when used properly.

---

[2]Mara Der Hovanesian, "Nightmare Mortgages," *Businessweek* (10 September 2006): www.businessweek.com/stories/2006-09-10/nightmare-mortgages.

The rationale for creating the option ARM goes back to the 1970s, when the macroeconomy presented lenders with a problem: The cost of funds was not only going up; it was also highly volatile, which made FRMs highly risky because the revenue to the lender was fixed. In the early 1980s, lenders were paying double digit rates to depositors to finance loans made a few years prior, which brought in only 6 percentage points of income. Lenders thus needed loans that could respond to changes in their cost of funds, but consumer groups at the time, as now, were worried that consumers could not handle floating rates.

A regional bank, Wachovia, came up with a solution in 1980: a mortgage called a "capped payment ARM," on which the interest payment fluctuated every month but the payments changed only once a year and could only rise 7.5% a year. It worked this way: The monthly payment was fixed on an annualized basis, using the current loan balance. Out of that payment, the lender first collected interest and then allocated the rest to pay down the principal. If the interest rate went up, more of the payment was allocated to interest and less to principal, and vice versa if the interest rate went down. The capped payment ARM thus gave the banks what they wanted (a mortgage in which the interest rate could fluctuate), and it gave consumers what they wanted (a fixed payment).

There is one important detail that, eventually, led to the loan's bad reputation. If the interest rate went really high, the interest could exceed the monthly payment. That is, not only was there not enough cash flow to pay down any principal; there wasn't even enough to pay the interest. But the capped payment ARM had a solution to this problem, which we call "negative amortization": To cover the shortfall in interest, the lender would *add* to the balance of the loan.

In a sense, the capped payment ARM is exactly what an economist would want—a loan that allows the borrower to smooth consumption and to behave just as the permanent income hypothesis suggests. When the interest rate is high, the loan allows the household to borrow against future income, and when the interest rate is low, the loan forces the borrower to save by allocating more money to pay down principal.

It was only later, when interest rates stabilized, that banks found another use for this product, which was to create a loan with an exceptionally low monthly payment for an extended period of time. Along with the new role came a new name: the option ARM. To turn a capped payment ARM into an option ARM, lenders made one major innovation. For the first month of the loan, the bank sets the interest rate fictitiously low—say, to 2%—which gives the borrower a fully amortizing monthly payment divided into principal and interest for the first month based on the low (2%) rate. Then, in the second month, the interest goes up to the market rate, and the borrower starts negatively amortizing. In other words, negative amortization was no longer just there for times when interest rates went up; it was a more or less permanent state of affairs.

Were option ARMs a problem product? In some sense, the answer is yes. A borrower could, in theory, make more than the minimum payment and pay off some of the balance or pay all the interest. But almost no one did that; most borrowers just made the minimum payment and added to their balance every month, a strategy that works well only if house prices are rising.

But something interesting happened during the crisis: Interest rates started falling. Interest rates eventually got so low that these borrowers actually started amortizing again. Even though they were making only the minimum payment, by 2009, these borrowers were paying off their mortgages. The perceived problem with option ARMs was that borrowers were adding to the balance, but the low interest rates associated with the financial crisis meant that these borrowers started paying off their mortgages in early 2009.

So, despite the fact that negative amortization more or less ceased by mid-2009, option ARMs defaulted in large numbers. Indeed, the performance of loans just kept getting worse and worse and worse. To explain their poor performance one must turn to the origination of these loans and conclude that something was wrong with the underwriting. That, and not the design of the loan, is where the problems happened. It wasn't that these loans were a time bomb that exploded. The borrowers just kept getting more and more delinquent throughout the crisis and continued to do so even when they started actually paying off the loan.

The option ARM is a tricky product to malign because there are some things about it that an economist will appreciate. Because of the historical negative relationship between short-term interest rates and unemployment, the option ARM plays an insurance role. That is, the cost of funds implicit in the loan varies inversely with the unemployment risk faced by the borrower. In other words, as things got worse in the economy, the payments borrowers made went down.

To sum up, the portrayal of adjustable-rate mortgages as villains in the crisis is incorrect, and therefore, the focus of the CFPB in informing borrowers about the contractual details of the mortgage contract is misplaced. There is little evidence that the crisis would have unfolded differently from the way it did if rather than informing borrowers of the details of their ARMs in 2005 we had simply banned them.

House Prices and Foreclosures

As should be clear by now, I do not think the information in the CFPB disclosure about changes in payments is very useful. I do not think most option ARM borrowers, had they known exactly how the payments were going to change, would have made any different decisions from the ones they did make.

And it is not clear that if they had gotten fixed-rate mortgages instead, they would have been any better off. The issue, for most borrowers, was house prices. Without falling house prices, there would have been no crisis.

In **Figure 1**, the top line is a plot of foreclosures in Massachusetts going back to the early 1990s and the middle line is a plot of house prices. It is important to understand what did not happen. Some people think that a lot of borrowers got into trouble, which pushed house prices down, but that is not what happened. As you can see, we have had episodes of high delinquency before, but delinquencies do not turn into foreclosures unless house prices are falling. In the 2001 recession, for example, we had a huge increase in delinquency in Massachusetts. But the foreclosure rate actually went down because house prices were rising and continued to rise through that recession.

I am not saying that underwriting was not a problem in the crisis; it was. But it is important to understand exactly the extent of that problem. In **Figure 2**, the bottom, solid black line represents actual foreclosures for borrowers who bought houses in 2002. The top, gray line represents actual foreclosures for borrowers who bought in 2005. The dotted and dashed lines show the number of foreclosures expressed as the probability of foreclosure for a borrower who

Figure 1.   Foreclosures and House Prices in Massachusetts, 1989–Present

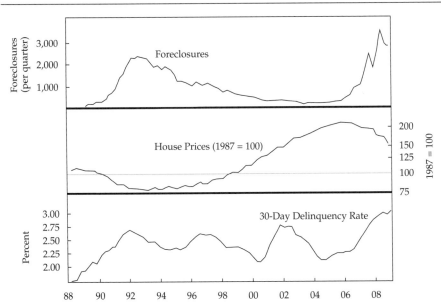

Source: Based on data from the Federal Reserve Bank of Boston, the Warren Group, and the Mortgage Bankers Association.

Figure 2. Role of House Prices in Causing Foreclosures in Massachusetts

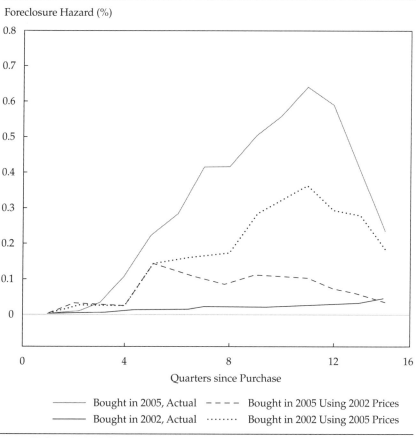

Foreclosure Hazard (%)

Quarters since Purchase

———————— Bought in 2005, Actual   – – – – Bought in 2005 Using 2002 Prices
———————— Bought in 2002, Actual   ········ Bought in 2002 Using 2005 Prices

Source: K. Gerardi, A.H. Shapiro, and P.S. Willen, "Decomposing the Foreclosure Crisis: House Price Depreciation versus Bad Underwriting," working paper (2009).

bought at a given time, in this case 2002 or 2005. For the people who bought in 2002, the foreclosure probability was less than 1/20 of 1%. For those who bought in 2005, it was several orders of magnitude higher.

Then we conducted a simulation to see how important underwriting was. We first asked, "What would have happened to the 2005 borrowers if they had gotten 2002 prices?" For the 2005 borrowers, the underwriting is clearly much looser, or more generous. About 20% of these borrowers had subprime loans when they bought, and 30% of them put zero down. And yet we see very few foreclosures in the simulation where they got 2002 prices (dashed line). Why? House prices were going up.

In contrast, the 2002 borrowers, where the underwriting was much less generous, had few subprime loans (fewer than 3% were subprime), and the percentage of borrowers using zero down was also much lower. But in the simulation where they paid 2005 house prices (dotted line), we see a big increase in foreclosures. Would this have been as bad a crisis if we had had more careful underwriting in 2005? Absolutely not. It would have been a much milder crisis, but it still would have been a crisis because house prices were falling so dramatically.

Alternative Mortgage Disclosure Form

Because we do not believe that knowing about changes in payments covers the true risks of a mortgage, we have proposed an alternate disclosure form. First, we rearranged the form to focus attention on house prices. Borrowers need to understand that when they buy a house, they are taking on an enormous amount of house price risk. What people needed to know about in 2005 was not that their mortgage payment might go up but that their house price could go down. The form says, "The appraised value of your home is $275,000." One question would be, "Does that mean I can sell my house for $275,000?" The answer is no. It means that you found an appraiser who was willing to say that $275,000 was a reasonable number. More to the point, it means you bid $275,000.

Another question is, "Will I always be able to sell my house for $275,000?" The answer is no. House prices can fall a lot. Another question would be, "Can house prices fall by 30% or more?" The answer to that question is yes. If house prices fall by 30%, you may have a house that is worth less than the outstanding balance of your mortgage. If you want to sell the house because you need to move, you might have to come up with some money to cover that difference. It is this information that people needed to know in 2005, not that their payment could go up.

The real issue is finding a clear way to convey to people what the risk is of taking out a mortgage. One of the exercises we did early in the crisis was to look at the probability that a borrower would lose his or her house to foreclosure over various horizons. We found that the median, prime homebuyer, if she bought her house over the next 10 years, had about a 3% chance of losing her home to foreclosure. A subprime borrower had an 18% chance.

Instead of giving elaborate descriptions of what might happen to house prices, we propose including some simple numbers, such as foreclosure rates, that people can understand. For example, the form could say, "Based on the information about this mortgage, we estimate that the probability you will lose this house to foreclosure is 5%. If house prices fall by 20%, the chance you will lose this house to foreclosure is 25%."

These estimates certainly depend on what inputs are used and how foreclosure is modeled. But this analysis gives borrowers, in a sense, exactly the same information that an investor would want—scenario analysis. What is the chance that something will go wrong with this investment? A borrower can understand that number. And for a refinancing, the idea would be to include something that says, "Here is your probability of default on this loan." And consequently, we would be able to say, for example, that the probability of losing this home to foreclosure, because of the refinanced loan that you have, is 2%. A crisp, clear number is something a borrower can actually use.

Conclusion

Part of the tragedy of the *Titanic* was that it did not have enough lifeboats for all the people on board. So after the sinking, there was much debate about the optimal number of lifeboats. Eventually someone said, "The optimal number of lifeboats is the number needed for everybody to get off the boat." And in fact, the rules were changed so that you had to have enough lifeboats to make sure that everybody could get off the boat, plus some extras.

What worries me about what we're doing right now with the CFPB proposed disclosure is that it is akin to saying, "We are not going to regulate how many lifeboats you need to have on a ship. What is important is that the shipping line must tell you how many lifeboats are on the boat when you buy a ticket. You can then make an informed choice and draw your own conclusions about the chances of the boat sinking."

I think in the end, disclosure is useful, but we should not delude ourselves into thinking that we could have prevented millions or even hundreds of thousands of foreclosures had we had a better disclosure form in 2005. It is possible that, in the end, if foreclosure prevention is our goal, we must make politically unpalatable choices to restrict the availability of mortgage credit.

Session 2: Housing Decisions: Do Consumers Know What They Need to Know?

Discussion

Karl E. Case, Moderator
Professor Emeritus of Economics
Wellesley College

Christopher Mayer
Senior Vice Dean and Paul Milstein Professor of Real Estate
Columbia Business School

Robert I. Lerman
Institute Fellow in Labor and Social Policy
Urban Institute
Professor of Economics
American University

Karl Case

First of all, it is certainly correct that default losses are limited as long as house prices do not fall. After all, houses are the collateral that stand behind mortgage loans. In general, house prices are sticky downward.

In the 1980s, Paul Volcker was chairman of the Fed and Ronald Reagan was president of the United States. Volcker put both feet on the monetary brakes, and the fed funds rate went to 22.9% in the middle of 1981. The Fed was no longer doing interest rate targeting; it was doing money supply targeting.

Among the most interesting events of that remarkable time are the developments in the housing markets. California had just had a huge boom. Then the interest rate increase hit, and everyone expected the housing market to collapse. But housing prices in California never fell. Demand dropped, and because the market was still dominated by fixed-rate, self-amortizing mortgages, homeowners did not want to sell in that environment. So, supply dropped as quickly as demand did in existing markets, but prices never fell in nominal terms. They went flat. In Vancouver, British Columbia, however, where interest rates went up to 22.9%, house prices fell 60% in the year and a half following the price index peak in 1981.

Thus, in two seemingly identical interest rate environments, California house prices went flat and Vancouver prices fell 60%. The difference was that Commonwealth countries, such as Canada, did not have fixed-rate mortgages. They had five-year adjustable mortgages. When interest rates went up, big adjustments took place and people could not make the payments. In that environment, borrowers and lenders both had risk associated with increases in interest rates.

The crash in the United States that began nationally in late 2005 taught us that prices *can* fall. The real question is under what circumstances do house prices *actually* fall.

Christopher Mayer

This is a historic time for mortgage finance because it gives us an opportunity to ask whether we can improve the way we do things. After all, we have to do something. Sooner or later, the federal government will no longer be backing 90–95% of all mortgages underwritten in the United States. All sides seem to agree on this point.

Improving the System, Aligning Incentives. The evidence presented by Paul Willen strongly supports the contention that misleading terms were probably not the principal cause of mortgage defaults during the housing crisis. I put more emphasis on poor underwriting. According to Willen's data simulations, we would have seen half the defaults and foreclosures had the market used the underwriting standards that prevailed in 2002 instead of those that prevailed in 2005. That is the glass-half-full interpretation of Willen's work.

In addition, we should examine the incentives facing not just consumers but also originators and lenders. Aligning incentives on both sides will help prevent future crises. Mortgage investors do not want to be stuck with bad investments any more than homeowners want to lose their homes, so working through the financial intermediation system is an important place to start making changes.

A few observations shed further light on the connection between underwriting standards and the crisis. A comparison of median cumulative-loan-to-value (CLTV) ratios and median FICO scores suggests that people who took out short-term hybrids were much lower-quality borrowers than those who took out fixed-rate mortgages (see **Table 1**).

The difference between a 627 and a 612 FICO score is quite predictive of default in those two groups. If house prices had kept going up, we would not have seen a lot of defaults, but as things worked out, defaults were plentiful and occurred most among those homebuyers who made very low down payments. From 2005 to 2007, the median CLTV ratio for purchasing rather

Table 1.   Attributes of Various Mortgage Types: 2003–2007

	Collateral Type	Fixed Rate	Floating Rate	Long-Term Hybrid	Short-Term Hybrid
Median CLTV	Subprime	80	90	85	89.47
	Alt-A	80	80	84.28	90
Median FICO	Subprime	627	625	660	612
	Alt-A	708	703	710	694

Source: Based on data from Christopher Mayer, Karen Pence, and Shane M. Sherlund, "The Rise in Mortgage Defaults," *Journal of Economic Perspectives,* vol. 23, no. 1 (Winter 2009):27–50.

than refinancing among subprime mortgages was 100%—that is, zero down. As soon as house prices started falling even a little bit, these borrowers walked away. They walked away, in fact, even before the unemployment rate started rising appreciably.

Consider early payment defaults (i.e., defaults within 12 months of origination). Among subprime mortgages originating in 2004, early payment defaults were less than 2%. By 2007, among subprime mortgages originating in that year, 8% of them went into early payment default. And these data are from 12 months after the first half of 2007, not 12 months after the second half, when the U.S. economy took a dramatic turn for the worse.

The homeownership rate peaked in the fourth quarter of 2004, so over the period when lending practices were at their worst (2005–2007), the homeownership rate was actually declining. Many of the people who were taking mortgages out at that time were investors or speculators. But that is the sort of thing that happens when you offer people loans with no money down.

Correcting Inefficiencies in the Mortgage Market. Mortgage financing in the United States has several inefficiencies that have led us to costly defaults and foreclosures. By aligning incentives properly, we might prevent some of these problems. For example, by reducing the subsidies for owner occupancy, we would encourage a more viable rental market, which would help balance the mortgage market.

■ *Refinancing and the efficacy of prepayment penalties.* Another area of inefficiency, and the one I will focus on, is refinancing. Some people may find this a peculiar choice, but the reality is that many bad loans originated not in purchasing but in refinancing. People owned a home, lived in that home, took on additional debt, paid high refinancing fees, and then defaulted. I consider this a serious problem associated with the crisis.

During the past decade, in fact, the number of refinancings was consistently larger (aside from 2006) than the number of purchase loans, even as interest rates were rising. Many homeowners, therefore, were pulling money out of their homes, paying the upfront fees associated with refinancing, and frequently taking on amounts of leverage they could neither manage nor afford.

This is a uniquely U.S. phenomenon. In many parts of the world, borrowers are not allowed to refinance their mortgages whenever they please. Other parts of the world also do not have such incredibly well-compensated mortgage brokers who take tens of billions of dollars in transaction fees. From 2003 to 2005, 27 million mortgages were refinanced in the United States. If we assume that each homeowner spent several thousand dollars to complete each refinancing and that the least sophisticated people were spending the most money, then we see that an enormous amount of money was taken from relatively less wealthy households so they could lever their finances in ways that did not make sound fiscal sense. This process clearly works in favor of more sophisticated households and against less sophisticated households.

One way to deter this misuse of refinancing is to assess prepayment penalties. I realize that prepayment penalties are poorly regarded in mortgage finance, but so are subprime loans, and both have an economic justification. For one thing, prepayment penalties promote a kind of risk sharing. Consider a pool of borrowers who all take out loans. All the loans represent a similar level of risk, but some of the borrowers end up doing well while others fare poorly. If the borrowers who do well are allowed to pay off their mortgages and drop out of the loan pool, the only people left in the pool are those who have done poorly. (The situation is similar to health insurance. If healthy people are allowed to opt out of the insurance pool, the only people left are sick people, who then have to be charged higher premiums.)

Thus, prepayment penalties discourage borrowers from leaving the pool and encourage more viable risk sharing among borrowers. Such penalties allow for *ex ante* risk sharing, which is a good thing because it allows us to help relatively disadvantaged borrowers. Many other countries have mortgages that are not prepayable, and they have not seen the same level of housing troubles that we have. If one were going to test the hypothesis that a 30-year fixed-rate mortgage with no prepayment penalty is really safe, the evidence from our experience in the United States would be unlikely to support the hypothesis. Yet during this crisis, the United States consistently resisted learning from the rest of the world.

The Fed has rules right now that limit prepayment penalties, and Fannie Mae and Freddie Mac will not enforce the penalties. So, it is virtually impossible to get this kind of innovation into the market. Nevertheless, we should be giving it serious consideration.

■ *Addressing foreclosures.* Dealing with the current glut of foreclosures has generated a number of interesting ideas. Robert Shiller and others have talked about continuous workout mortgages and home equity insurance. I like the idea of enforcing minimum down payment requirements. If we think defaults are risky and costly, maybe we should require people to put money down on their mortgages. Such action would address the externality of falling house prices due to mortgages spiraling down. As for home equity insurance, I think that the people who have priced it have been wrong in their calculations by an order of magnitude because paying someone to bear additional mortgage risk after this crisis would cost a lot of money. After all, we do not even want the banks to bear such additional risk because we do not want to have to bail them out again.

I think these self-correcting mortgages, in which the lenders effectively bear all of the house price risk, are too expensive. A down payment, however—an instrument that requires more equity from homeowners—achieves the same goal.

■ *Reducing subsidies for homeownership.* Finally, we need to question why we are giving such big subsidies to homeowners. Most people probably nod their heads in agreement when the issue is raised, but nothing ever happens, which I think is a big mistake. After all, much of that subsidy does not result in higher homeownership. The United States has about the same homeownership rate as the typical OECD (Organisation for Economic Co-Operation and Development) country. Most of the subsidy just encourages excess housing consumption and more leverage—two things that we hardly want to encourage through the tax code.

Perhaps, instead, we should think about tax credits or matching programs for down payments. Those would be good ways to help low-income households. It is hard to get people to save for the future, but some evidence from Canada suggests that we can do a better job helping people save to buy a home by matching down payments for three years. This policy takes advantage of the evidence on savings and ways to encourage savings, and it also gets around the hyperbolic discounting problem in a way that might be effective at increasing the savings rates for lower- to moderate-income households.

Summary. We do have solutions to help fix the problems with mortgage financing, even if some of them seem counterintuitive. I think we should (1) reduce access to costly refinancing because it encourages the least sophisticated households to make complicated decisions for big stakes, (2) prevent inefficient levels of foreclosures, (3) align incentives, and (4) reduce the subsidy for homeownership.

Karl Case

I would like to point out that the refinance boom in the middle of the past decade was related to the Fed's reduction of short-term interest rates to prevent more damage from the events of 2001. Rates were dropped from about 6% to under 2% in a period of less than a year. The resulting refinance boom was enormous. According to Alan Greenspan and James Kennedy, a trillion dollars in refinancing occurred in the third quarter of 2003.[1] The United States, in effect, refinanced its entire book of mortgages, $10 trillion, over the three or four years of the boom. And the resulting fees during that time were also immense.

Then, in the middle of 2003, the long-term interest rate spiked and the refinance boom ended. The mortgage originators who had been collecting those outsized refinancing fees went looking for new buyers.

Robert Lerman

As a member of the Urban Institute, my work is centered on benefit programs in the low-income population, and those programs, I believe, can provide insight into a plan that could reinvigorate the housing sector in a way that is efficient and has long-term logic.

To begin, consider two people who each buy a house for $180,000 with a mortgage of $160,000. Real estate values boom, and the value of the two homes goes up to $300,000 each. One person keeps his $160,000 mortgage; the other person takes out a loan and raises her mortgage to $270,000. Then the real estate bubble bursts, and the value of the two homes drops to $200,000 each. The person who did not take out the extra mortgage can continue making his payments and is still ahead of the game. The person who refinanced is underwater.

Events such as these leave us in the situation of subsidizing the mistakes of homeowners, but we are ambivalent about doing so. Yet there are equity and efficiency considerations that we have not considered, and it is from this perspective that I am going to propose an alternative. But before offering my proposal, let me present some background data.

Homeownership and Rent Subsidies. First, low-income people do own houses. As of 2007, 43% of people in the bottom quartile of income were homeowners. Fifty-three percent of single parents and high school dropouts owned homes. The median value of homes owned by those in the bottom two quintiles of income was $100,000–$120,000.

The interest burdens among low-income households, however, are very high. Thus, if low-income homeowners could refinance or have lower risk at the beginning, they could save a lot of money.

Second, rents have increased nearly 4% since January 2008. Furthermore, actual subsidies for low-income people in the housing sector are oriented predominantly toward rent rather than homeownership, although the Federal

---

[1]Alan Greenspan and James Kennedy, "Sources and Uses of Equity Extracted from Homes," *Oxford Review of Economic Policy*, vol. 24, no. 1 (Spring 2008):120–144.

Housing Administration does insure certain mortgages. Unfortunately, we provide very rich subsidies for a small group of renters—about 28% of eligible renters—and zero for the rest.

The result is that large numbers of families are stuck on rent subsidy waiting lists that take years to clear, thus leaving huge segments of the low-income population with big rent burdens. Large numbers of people are paying over 50% of their incomes on shelter.

Homeownership Subsidy Program. Because of the downturn in the economy, unemployment has gone up. At the same time, a lot of low-income people are paying huge amounts on rent even as house prices have dropped dramatically. I suggest we can address both problems with a single proposal patterned on our rent voucher program, which is to fund 1 million new homeownership vouchers. Doing so would both raise the demand for owner-occupied housing and help low-income families.

The program would call for a guarantee—in income maintenance terms—stating that the maximum payment a homebuyer would pay would be the fair market rent in each community or a lower amount. For those of you who are not familiar with the housing subsidy system, the fair market rent is equal to rent at the 40th percentile of the local community's rate. If the 40th percentile in a community is $1,000 a month, participants receive vouchers that allow them to buy rental services for $1,000 a month and they pay 30% of their income to buy the vouchers. If a participant has an income of $1,000 a month, he pays $300 for a $1,000 rent voucher. If he has an income of $2,000 a month, he pays $600. Because the subsidy is a percentage, it rises and falls with the participant's income.

I recommend expanding this program to the owner-occupied sector but limiting it to areas where prices are way down. We could establish the fair market rent or the carrying cost of low-cost homes, which I would set at the 25th income percentile. This level is actually quite generous because people who own at the 25th percentile have incomes that are considerably higher than people who rent at the 40th percentile of rent. The house they buy would probably be an upgrade.

◼ *Special features of the program.* Certain special features would have to be considered. For example, not only the home price but also the cost of maintenance and repairs would have to be accounted for. Perhaps participants would have to complete homeownership training and put money into escrow on a monthly basis for repairs. Thus, financial literacy would be linked to homeownership.

The program could also include a recoupment plan. Because the government would be helping to finance these mortgages for low-income people through a direct subsidy, it might be appropriate for the government to share in any capital gain experienced by the owners and thus recoup some of the funding.

■ *Why such a program can work.* For those who doubt that such a program could work in today's market, I would point out that fair market rents today are higher than the monthly carrying cost of homes, often by big margins. Consider, for example, Riverside, California, where the home value at the 25th percentile of home prices was $108,000 in mid-2010. The fair market rent in Riverside for a three bedroom apartment or house—that is, the maximum subsidy that HUD (U.S. Department of Housing and Urban Development) provides to someone who is getting a rent voucher—was $1,044 per month. The monthly carrying cost on the 25th percentile house—which includes interest, taxes, insurance, and some amount for maintenance—would have been only $650 per month. If the participant were earning a relatively small amount (say, $9 an hour), working 80% of the year, and receiving the earned income credit, 30% of this person's income would come to $460 a month. That is her cash contribution to her $1,044 rent voucher, leaving the government to pay the $584 difference. Her contribution to the $650 cost of the mortgage and other expenses would also be $460. But now, the government would only pay the $190 difference. So, the net cost to the government of putting low-income people into houses that they own would be less than $200 per month per home—far less than the cost of expanding the rent voucher program. Such a program would help a lot of low-income people while also increasing the demand for housing. And it would achieve both goals at a much lower cost.

Furthermore, house prices at the 25th percentile in the United States as a whole are actually lower than Riverside prices, and the cost of the rent voucher is also somewhat lower. The two tend to go together. As house prices at the 25th percentile go up, so do rents and rent vouchers. In almost all geographical areas, the rent is enough to support the monthly carrying costs of buying. Frequently, the carrying cost of ownership is much lower than the rent.

■ *Advantages of a homeownership subsidy program.* Such a program offers several advantages. First, we can increase the number of low-income households that can afford adequate housing. Second, the program would limit price downturns in neighborhoods hit by high levels of foreclosures. Third, the program would provide for financial education at the point of key decision making. Fourth, we could increase the demand for owner-occupied housing. Fifth, the program would lock in the unit cost of the housing subsidies because a mortgage payment is fixed whereas rent increases. Based on the history of the rent voucher system, once participants get a rent voucher, they keep it indefinitely; the federal government has to keep raising the amount in the program to keep it at the 40th percentile of rent. But a mortgage subsidy will lock in the government's monthly payment.

Finally, the cost of my proposed program can be offset by phasing down or phasing out the low-income housing tax credit, which is paid to developers. The cost of my program would be $2 billion to $3 billion a year. The low-income housing tax credit is a supply-oriented subsidy. It is intended to expand supply, which is not needed now. Furthermore, it is unclear whether the tax credit even does an effective job of expanding supply. By phasing out the low-income housing tax credit and adding the cost of my program, the federal government would actually end up saving money—$5 billion a year by 2019.

Karl Case

Based on what is happening in the housing market today, a program such as this proposal will face a lot of resistance. Housing production is at its lowest level in 60 years, and it seems to be staying there, despite the fact that the vacancy rate is still high, although down somewhat from its peak. The rental vacancy rate is about 10.6%, and the owner-occupied rate is 2.6% or 2.7%. Historically, as housing production adjusts, vacancy rates come down because household formation runs ahead of new units. For example, a typical housing production peak is 2.3 million or 2.4 million new units per year. When production drops below 1 million, vacancy rates usually come down. For five cycles it did that. Now, for 33 months, it has been stuck around 500,000.

The government is in favor of owner-occupied housing. Consider the advantages of buying a home outright. Homeownership offers a good return. The income or "dividend" from it is the imputed rent, the value of services the owner gets by living in the house, which is tax free.

If owners want to finance their homes, they have access to interest rates that are effectively being held to zero, in part by quantitative easing and in part by expansive monetary policy. A homebuyer today can get a mortgage interest rate below 4%. For those who itemize, the 4% comes down to 2% after taxes, which is just about zero in the historical context. And owners are getting this financing in the presence of tax-free income from that property. It is amazing how big a subsidy is being poured into housing.

Rentals have certainly been the underdog in this battle for 30 years, but it will be hard to do much on either side of this issue. When anybody mentions repealing the mortgage deduction, builders, realtors, and mortgage bankers get on the telephone and call their representatives in Congress.

Question and Answer Session

Question: Are Americans putting too much money into a home and not enough into retirement savings?

Willen: If you look at people who retired in the early 1990s, particularly low- and middle-income individuals, housing was their predominant source of wealth, unless they got some kind of pension. With the current wave of both refinancing and home equity borrowing, many more people are arriving at retirement age with debts on their home, which fundamentally changes the retirement calculation. That is, we've made it easier for people to hit retirement without the big source of saving that they used to have, which was a fully amortized mortgage.

Case: Or a house that is rising in value. If you calculate the savings rate as including capital gains, which is the way a lot of people think about income—consumption plus change in net worth—the increase in housing value is savings from a household's standpoint. From society's, though, it is just inflation in the value of existing assets.

Lerman: When people arrive at retirement with their mortgages paid off, they have zero monthly payments, although they still have to pay property taxes, which can be high, and insurance. Even so, they have cut way down on expenses. Furthermore, they have the option of turning their capital asset, a paid-for house, into cash flow. That's where reverse mortgages can play a role, although with interest rates this low, I'm not sure that anyone wants to jump into a reverse mortgage right now.

So, I don't see a preponderance of wealth in homeownership as a big problem. People can enjoy their houses, and their expenses have gone down.

Question: In a world without inflation to build the value of a house, should adjustments be made, other than the size of down payments, to reduce the riskiness of mortgages and build value in the house, perhaps by adjusting the rate of payment on mortgages?

Willen: Yes. In the early 1980s, fixed-rate mortgages with accelerating inflation were amortizing very quickly. People were paying off their loans. But that was a development heavily influenced by inflation. Many homeowners are under the misconception that their mortgage payments are immediately beginning to pay off their loan. But without inflation, not much amortization occurs early on, as anybody who's refinanced after owning a house for five years can tell you. Homeowners are often shocked by how little they have paid off after five years.

Case: Unfortunately, over the past few years and in most parts of the country, amortization has been dwarfed by the leveraged returns on houses. If a couple buys a house with 10% down, 10% appreciation doubles their money but 10% depreciation takes it to zero. The gains and losses amounting to $10 trillion over a period of 10 years because of house price fluctuations dwarf amortization. But buying a house today with a new, fixed-rate mortgage at today's low rates can still be a good investment, even without appreciation. If the payment goes down over time in real terms, the buyer is in good shape.

Question: Do you think prepurchase homebuyer education programs reduce the sort of leveraging that leads to foreclosures?

Mayer: I have seen no studies that randomize on providing financial education. I have seen one study done in Chicago that essentially fell apart because after prepurchase education was offered, the participants chose not to buy homes.

I am certainly willing to believe that education is useful, but typically the participants who receive the education and those who do not are not randomly selected, which makes it hard to draw conclusions.

Question: My experience with the Housing Network of Rhode Island leads me to believe that prepayment penalties increase the likelihood of default and were a factor in the credit crisis. What do you think?

Mayer: The issue is not whether people with prepayment penalties got into trouble disproportionately. The question should be, Did those specific characteristics cause the defaults in some meaningful way?

For a prepayment penalty to cause higher defaults, one would have to argue that, had they not been facing prepayment penalties, borrowers would have been able to refinance their mortgages. I have seen little evidence to support that argument.

Furthermore, even if it were true, one would have to go back to the beginning, when the borrowers took out their mortgages. If they had taken out mortgages without prepayment penalties, they would have had to pay higher rates, which might have caused other difficulties. After controlling for other variables, I have found no evidence that prepayment penalties cause defaults. If anything, defaults were slightly lower in mortgages with these penalties.

One possible reason is that people who took them out got the benefit of lower rates. Furthermore, many nations around the world—including Canada and many European nations—have both prepayment penalties and enormously stable housing and mortgage markets.

Session 3: Credit Decisions: Do Consumers Know What They Need to Know?

The Credit Counseling Industry— Distinguishing between the Reputable and the Less Reputable

William Samuelson, Moderator
Professor
Boston University School of Management

Mel Stiller
President
Money Management International of Massachusetts

I have been asked to give a presentation on the credit counseling industry— what a reputable agency looks like and how to find one, as well as what the challenges have been for the credit counseling industry for the past 20 or so years because of competition. The lines have been blurred in the credit counseling industry for a long time. Those of you who are up watching television in the early hours of the morning have probably seen the commercials that have given all of us involved with credit counseling a bad name. To better understand how and why these entities appeared on the landscape, it will be helpful to understand how and why the legitimate agencies came into being.

Origins of Credit Counseling

Although credit itself goes back to the very beginnings of the country, credit cards are a relatively recent piece of our credit history. And in the 1950s and 1960s, as credit and credit products began to flourish as never before, so did the accompanying problems. The social services community started seeing problems as financial issues began to get tied in with all sorts of social and medical problems. The consumer movement was coming to the forefront, and it began to identify problems associated with credit card use, as did governmental agencies. And the credit-granting community itself was experiencing delinquencies as a result of the abuse of, and lack of education around, credit cards. And so throughout the country, these entities worked together to form nonprofit credit counseling agencies that would operate with the purpose of both resolving and preventing financial problems. For example, here in the Boston area we had a wide variety of agencies and institutions involved with forming our agency and serving on our board of directors during those important, formative years. The Massachusetts Consumers' Council, the Boston Consumers' Council, the Better Business Bureau, the Federal Trade Commission, the Federal Deposit Insurance Corporation (FDIC), the Department of Consumer Affairs, and other nonprofits, such as the Family Service Association, joined with financial institutions, retailers, and employers to give support and direction to us.

Role of Legitimate Agencies

So, what does and what should a legitimate credit counseling agency do? Primarily, it does three things: education, counseling, and debt management.

Education. By education, I am talking about group education programs, where we talk to people of all ages about issues around credit, debt, budgeting, and money management. For example, at our agency we have programs geared toward young children, where we talk to them about the difference between wants and needs; toward high school and college students, where we might talk about the principles around credit use or car purchases; toward both younger and older adults, where we talk about managing credit or buying a home; and to seniors, where we might talk about frauds and scams, identity theft, or reverse mortgages.

Good credit counseling agencies will not only hold their own programs but also partner with others—employers, social service agencies, government entities, financial institutions—to help reach a wide variety of people. They will be entrenched in their communities, serving on advisory boards or partnering with other educational organizations, such as the Jump$tart Coalition.[1] And they will have websites with great financial education resources, such as articles and calculators.

Counseling. The other major piece is the counseling side. Let me say at the outset that the counseling side is not just for those having difficulty making ends meet. I know when you think of credit counseling, you associate it with people having problems. And human nature being what it is, most people wait until they are having problems before meeting with a counselor. But a good credit counseling agency will be there to serve those who just want an objective

---

[1]See jumpstart.org.

look at their budget, those who want to better understand their credit reports, those who just bought a home and want some post-purchase direction, and those who want to meet a financial goal, such as saving more.

But for the purposes of this discussion, I will concentrate on what happens in a counseling session for those who are having a financial problem. I will do that not just because they represent the vast majority of those we counsel but also because it leads into the story of our competition and how and why these competing entities developed.

When people with financial problems come in, the first thing we want to do, obviously, is set them at ease and establish trust. It is usually difficult to admit there is a problem and then come to a stranger and talk about it, so establishing that rapport is vital.

The next thing we try to do is get to the root cause of the problem. Often, the problem is poor decision making or an unfortunate circumstance, such as a job loss, but there are times when there are underlying issues: marital problems, substance abuse, gambling, or depression, to name a few. And while we are not marital counselors, or substance abuse counselors, or addiction counselors, or mental health counselors, our counselors do have resource directories at their side, and they try to steer clients toward the proper help for those underlying issues. This is vital because if there is an underlying issue, no matter what we do on the credit counseling side, we are unlikely to be successful unless that underlying cause is also being treated.

Next, we take a picture of what is coming in each month and compare it with what is going out. For most people, it is the first time they have ever undertaken that exercise. And yet, when you think about it, it is the most important thing you can do when making a spending decision. How can you tell if you're taking on too much car or too much house if you do not even know if there is a surplus or a deficit at the end of an average month? So, we break down spending into every possible category—not just the rent and food and insurance, but also the meals out, the haircuts, the morning coffee, the gifts, and those similar optional expenses that usually add up to hundreds of dollars a month for the average person.

At the end of that exercise we are able to compare an average month of income with an average month of expenses. And in most cases, there is a deficit. And in most cases, there is surprise on the other side of the desk.

The other part of taking a picture of current circumstances is looking at assets and liabilities. Most of our clients do not have assets to speak of, other than possibly a car or home, and there is often little equity there. The liabilities are usually substantial in relation to income, with credit card debt of around $25,000 compared with income of under $40,000 not being unusual.

So, our job is to help clients develop an action plan that will balance the budget and steer them on a path to getting the debts under control. And, as you would expect, the areas we look at are increasing income, reducing expenses, liquidating assets, and if possible and appropriate, reducing debt payments.

■ *Increasing income.* In terms of increasing income, we discuss a number of possibilities. We look at the paycheck and what happens between the gross and the net amounts to see if perhaps any of the deductions can be changed. For example, sometimes people take out too much in taxes so they can get a large refund when they may be better served by having that money in their checks each week. Sometimes we talk about the possibility of overtime or a part-time job for extra income, although those options are more difficult in an economy such as the current one.

Sometimes we talk about other possibilities, such as taking in boarders if there is room or having children who are working but living at home contribute to the family finances. Anything that could bring in extra income we discuss.

■ *Reducing expenses.* On the expense side, we go through the same exercise. We look back over the budget and ask if there are any expenses that can be reduced or eliminated. That may include small expenses, such as eliminating the coffee and bagel in the morning or taking a lunch instead of buying one each day. It could include suggestions like spending less at the holidays or reducing the amount of phone or cable features. Or it could be major lifestyle changes, such as eliminating one of the cars or switching to a less expensive occupancy situation.

■ *Liquidating assets.* Then we look at assets to see if there are any that could be sold to help reduce debt. As I said before, most of our clients are not in the situation where they have liquid assets that could help their situation; but still, it is something we look at.

And just to be clear, whether we are talking about increasing income, cutting expenses, or liquidating assets, it is never done in a preachy or judgmental manner. We present options and give clients ideas to think about, and the decisions are entirely up to them.

■ *Reducing debt payments.* And then, of course, there is the debt side. We examine the debts to see how much the client owes, what the interest rate is, and what the delinquency status is on each account. We look at some of the options around the debts. For example, is refinancing or consolidating a possibility? For most of our clients, this is not a viable option because they have already consolidated or refinanced themselves into a problem or because their credit score is such that they would not be approved even if it were a good option.

Is rewriting the terms of a loan to lower payments an option? Sometimes it is on fixed payment accounts, but for most of our clients, the problem is revolving credit lines. Is bankruptcy an option? We are not attorneys, but all of our clients are told about the bankruptcy option and advised to consult an attorney to learn more about it. I will talk more about that later. Or is a Debt Management Plan through our office a possibility? We find it is for approximately 25% of our debt counseling clients.

■ *Debt management.* A Debt Management Plan (or DMP) is appropriate when—after all of the suggestions are made and the client has considered ways of increasing income, decreasing expenses, and liquidating assets and thought through other debt options—we find there is money available each month for unsecured debt payment but not enough to meet the payments as currently constituted. For example, the client's unsecured debt payments may total $500 per month but we find, after comparing an average month's income with an average month's expenses, that there is only $350 per month available.

Under a DMP, we would negotiate with the creditors to try to get the payments reduced to that $350 amount, which would fit within the client's budget. The client would make a monthly deposit with us, and we, in turn, would disburse the funds proportionally to the creditors, usually over a period of three to five years. We would also try to negotiate lower interest rates (so that the client makes progress each month on the principal) and ask that over-limit fees and late charges be stopped. We ask that collection calls stop and that the lender call us going forward if there is a payment issue. One other benefit is that some creditors re-age accounts—that is, they set the client's payment to the new, lower payment we have proposed so that the client is not getting further behind.

So, the DMP can be a great product when appropriate. I say "when appropriate" because it is not fair to clients to set them up on DMPs when they cannot afford it—that is, when there is not enough money truly available in an average month to make the deposit to us affordable. And it is not fair to creditors to ask for all these concessions if the clients can handle the contractual payments on their own.

The clients have obligations under a DMP. They are expected to live on the budget we established with them. They are expected to get rid of their credit cards, with the exception of keeping one for business purposes when appropriate. They are expected to make regular deposits to our office and contact us if there is a problem. And they are expected not to apply for additional credit during the life of the program without first discussing it with us.

The final piece of a debt counseling session is to give the client the tools to prevent future problems—by that I mean discussing basic budgeting and money management skills.

Summary. I just want to reiterate that the process I have reviewed for you is for our debt counseling clients. I am focusing on them because the debt counseling process is what credit counseling agencies are most known for and it is a large part of what separates the reputable agencies from those less reputable.

But it is important to understand that a good credit counseling agency does more on the counseling side than just debt counseling. For example, our agency is approved by HUD to do housing counseling, and we have a strong mortgage delinquency counseling program and reverse mortgage counseling program. We are also approved by the Executive Office for United States Trustees to do pre-filing bankruptcy counseling and post-filing bankruptcy education. And as I mentioned earlier, we are available for preventative counseling, such as helping with budgeting or helping to reach a financial goal. But time precludes detailed descriptions of those programs because I need to get to what happened with competition in the credit counseling industry.

Increased Competition

Our competition has come in three waves, starting with the credit clinics.

Credit Clinics. The first wave of competition began approximately 20 years ago with the advent of "credit clinics." These companies promised to "clean up" a client's credit. For a hefty fee, paid in advance, they promised to eliminate negative information from the client's credit bureau report, even if it was truthful information. In reality, they were just challenging negative information. Regulations stated, and still state, that if information was challenged, the lender had to respond within a certain amount of time or else the information had to be removed from the report. What the credit clinics were banking on was that with enough persistence, the creditors might tire of the process or perhaps something would slip through the cracks, allowing the information to come off the report.

There were several problems with this. First, there is the moral issue of trying to get truthful information erased from a credit report so that the report is no longer an accurate reflection of one's credit history. Second, there is the fact that credit clinics were not doing anything that an individual could not do on his or her own. Third, the fees were large and usually had to be paid before services were rendered. And fourth, many promises were made by the credit clinics that could not be kept; no one can guarantee that a credit report will be cleaned up because no one can predict whether the lenders will diligently respond to the challenges.

It took a few years, but eventually, regulators began catching up with the credit clinics. Laws were put into effect whereby untrue statements could not be made by these companies and fees could not be taken in advance of rendering service. The new regulations helped quite a bit, and you do not hear as much about credit clinics now.

But the problem has not completely gone away; the Federal Trade Commission reached a settlement with a Florida credit clinic just a few months ago. It had been charged with doing things that the regulations were supposed to have stopped: making untrue promises and statements while charging large up-front fees for services that were not rendered. So, the problem continues, but at nowhere near the scale that it used to be.

How did this hurt the credit counseling industry if credit clinics do not do anything similar to what we are doing? The problem is that it started to plant seeds of distrust and confusion in the eyes of consumers. Our industry was mostly known as being "consumer credit counseling services" in those days; for example, our name was Consumer Credit Counseling Service of Massachusetts. The clinics started using a couple of the "consumer credit counseling service" words in their names. And the average consumer did not know the difference between a credit clinic and credit counseling agency. So, we were sometimes painted with the same negative brush, and some consumers did not get the help they needed because, as the negative publicity built, they could not distinguish the good guys from the bad guys.

The next problem that came about was from those who created a for-profit model based on what the nonprofits were doing. And to understand what happened, you need to understand how nonprofit credit counseling agencies are funded.

Nonprofit Funding Model. Most nonprofits have diverse funding models. We raise money through corporate and foundation grants. Some get United Way funding. There has been housing counseling revenue available through HUD for decades, but government income has really picked up the past few years for mortgage default counseling. Financial institutions and employers will usually pay us to do educational programs. And although our debt and budget counseling is free, we are allowed to charge for reverse mortgage counseling and bankruptcy counseling and education.

But a large and important piece of our funding has been through the Debt Management Plans that I spoke about earlier. Clients generally pay a monthly fee to a credit counseling agency for handling their unsecured debt payments. And the creditors who receive payments generally pledge back to credit counseling agencies a percentage of what they receive. A dozen or so years ago, the large national creditors, who received the bulk of the disbursements, were paying credit counseling agencies approximately 13% in what is known as "fair share" payments.

Let me stop here for a moment and address the inherent conflict of interest issue that plagues the credit counseling industry: Do agencies talk about solutions that might be looked at as anti-creditor—mainly, bankruptcy—when creditors provide a decent percentage of funding for nonprofit agencies? While the dreaded appearance of conflict is always there, many checks and balances are in place to ensure this does not happen: regulatory scrutiny, national association scrutiny, board scrutiny, and staff scrutiny. And staff scrutiny might not sound like scrutiny at all, but counselors would not stand for a minute to be paid nonprofit wages while feeling like they were not helping their clients.

Perhaps most important of all, bankruptcy information is usually given to consumers routinely by reputable agencies, even if bankruptcy does not make a lot of sense in a particular instance, just to avoid the appearance of a conflict. For example, I talked to my board of directors about this appearance of conflict back in the 1970s, and we adopted a policy that all clients who walk in the door receive written information about the bankruptcy option.

For-Profit Model. Getting back to the competition story, some enterprising individuals looked at our model and found a way to make a fortune, thus ushering in the second wave of competition. First, they only did debt management; they did not do the pieces for which there was little or no income stream. That means no counseling and no education. Second, they eliminated the major expense of in-person offices; services were only offered over the telephone. Third, they only spent approximately 20 minutes with clients, as opposed to the 60–90 minutes it would take a nonprofit counseling agency to do initial counseling sessions.

So, a counselor at an agency like ours might see four or five people a day and, with approximately one of four finding that a Debt Management Plan was the appropriate solution, set up one DMP per day. With the for-profit model, their so-called counselors made debt management the solution for everyone. Setting up a program every 20 minutes by phone enabled each of their employees to establish up to 24 DMPs in a day. Clients were paying high fees; creditors, at least at first, were paying fair share; and the money was rolling in to these companies. And while we were investing our revenues in branch offices and in education, they were putting theirs into television and radio advertising.

There were other problems with these companies. Sometimes debts were not paid at all. I cannot tell you how many clients came to our agency after having a negative experience with an entity that promised to pay creditors but did not.

Consumers, of course, did not understand the difference between the two models; they just wanted to get out of debt. To make matters worse, some of these organizations, like the credit clinics, made false promises, were not open in disclosing client fees, did not render the services promised, and increasingly used two and sometimes three of the words "consumer credit counseling service" in their own names.

What resulted, of course, was more confusion in the marketplace. Consumers were going to these companies in droves because of the advertising. Then, as negative publicity built toward these entities as complaints piled up and regulators started dealing with them, consumers started staying away from the reputable nonprofits because, again, they could not tell the good ones from the bad ones.

But the negative effect of these organizations on the reputable nonprofits was not just about confusion among consumers. These entities caused a landscape change that altered our industry forever.

Debt Management Plans were flooding the market. The cost to creditors of fair share payments was skyrocketing. And to make matters worse, national creditors were quickly merging, so the fair share cost for the merged entity was significantly higher than it was for the institutions prior to merger.

So, creditors started looking at the rates they were paying and began cutting them. And they have not stopped cutting them. The 13% rate of the mid- to late 1990s is down to approximately 4.5% today. Nonprofit agencies began looking for new revenue sources, but they were also forced to slash expenses. Mergers almost became the norm. Now, there are approximately half the number of agencies under our national umbrella organization (the National Foundation for Credit Counseling) as there used to be, and nearly half of those are not independent but rather part of multi-service agencies.

Another effect of the for-profit model was regulatory scrutiny. Some of the scrutiny was welcome and overdue. The Internal Revenue Service audited most of us, and that was a good thing. Those of us using the nonprofit model kept our 501(c)(3) tax exemption, and the process further weeded out those who did not deserve nonprofit status. In fact, when Ameridebt was shut down by the regulators, we were awarded its client base.

But other regulations have not been so good. For example, because excessive fees were a problem with the less reputable companies, states are now passing legislation that is too restrictive on fees.

So now, not only is funding down from creditors, but also our ability to ask reasonable fees of clients has been reduced in some states. And for agencies such as ours, which are approved to operate in every state, keeping up with and complying with so many different state regulations is very expensive and time-consuming.

Debt Settlement Companies. As the second wave of competition started to fade, the third wave came—debt settlement companies. Typically, debt settlement companies promise to negotiate with creditors to reduce the principal balance on debts, sometimes by as much as 70%. In exchange, the client typically pays an up-front fee that is a percentage of his or her outstanding balance.

In addition, clients are often required to set aside money in a separate account maintained by the debt settlement company. That money is supposed to be used to pay off the client's debt. Not surprisingly, regulators and Better Business Bureaus began receiving complaints about these companies. The complaints, in general, were that debts were not being paid off, clients were getting deeper in debt due to accruing interest, and they were being sued by the creditors.

There were other problems. Some of the companies would falsely say that the client's credit would not be affected. Most would advise not to make any payments to creditors while paying the settlement company but did not tell consumers what the implications of that would be. Some were not advising consumers that creditors were under no obligation to accept settlement terms. And some were not letting consumers know that forgiven debt could be taxable.

It took a while, but as with the other competitors, the regulators caught up with them. Some states have enacted laws regulating these companies. And under new Federal Trade Commission rules that went into effect a few months ago, most of these practices have to stop, at least for those who provide services by telephone.

First, debt settlement companies cannot collect up-front fees; they cannot get paid until services are rendered. The client now needs to agree in writing to the settlement agreements.

In addition, the accounts into which consumers put their money are no longer maintained by the debt settlement company. The funds must be placed in an independent financial institution under the client's name, with the client having the ability to withdraw the funds at any time, without penalty, or in an account administered by an independent third party.

There are also new disclosure rules. The settlement companies have to disclose to clients how long it will take to get results, how much it will cost, and what potential negative consequences could come from the process. In addition, there are rules against misrepresentations: They need to disclose whether or not they are a nonprofit and what their success rate is.

I feel there are a couple of problems with these rules that hopefully will be addressed. First, the rules need to be expanded beyond debt settlement services offered by telephone; providers who meet face-to-face with clients before signing them up are now exempt from most of the provisions. Second, the rules do not limit the amount of fees that companies can charge.

Summary. So, that is the story of the competition the legitimate non-profits have faced from those less reputable. I guess the good news in all of this is that the regulators do eventually catch up with most of those less reputable. The bad news, of course, is that it generally takes years for that to happen and large numbers of consumers get hurt in the meantime. Plus, many have been discouraged from seeking the help they need because they are confused as to which organizations they can trust.

Identifying a Trusted Source

So, that leads to the concluding part of this presentation: How do you know who to trust? I thought the most objective way of answering that question was to read what the Federal Trade Commission suggested in its piece *Fiscal Fitness: Choosing a Credit Counselor.* The FTC recommends asking the following:

- Does the organization offer a range of services rather than just debt management plans?

- Are educational materials available for free?

- Are the counselors certified?

- Will the agency send out free information or brochures describing the agency?

- Is in-person counseling an option?

- Will the agency help develop a plan not just to solve the immediate problem but also to avoid future problems?

- What are the fees?

- Will fees be waived or reduced if they are not affordable?

- Is the agency licensed?

- Will information be kept confidential?

- Are commissions paid to counselors if a debt management plan is established?

- Will options other than a DMP be discussed?

The FTC goes on to urge consumers to ask questions so that they have a thorough understanding of a DMP, such as how credit is affected, how finance charges are affected, and what other implications there may be. It urges consumers to check out the agency with a local Better Business Bureau, consumer protection agency, or state attorney general's office.

The FTC piece is good, and it touches on a lot of what I have been talking about here, including debt settlement and credit repair. It is easily found on the FTC's website.[2]

---

[2] See www.ftc.gov/bcp/edu/pubs/consumer/credit/cre26.shtm.

Conclusion

So, that is a quick overview of the nonprofit credit counseling industry, what it does, who its competitors are, and how the reputable agencies can be found. It is a challenging environment right now, probably the most challenging I have seen in the nearly 40 years I have been involved with credit counseling. Some of it is due to factors I have mentioned, such as increased regulation, reduced creditor support, and competition.

But some of it is due to factors I have not mentioned. For example, many in Congress now want to stop housing counseling funding while the volume of people needing help, particularly (ironically) those facing foreclosure and in need of housing counseling, remains high. And in an economy such as this, when many are without essential needs because of unemployment, credit counseling is a less likely candidate for foundation funding.

And one other factor making it a challenging environment is that solutions are not as readily available. As I stated earlier, options around increasing income, such as part-time jobs and overtime, are less viable in an environment such as this. Options like rewriting a mortgage or, in extreme cases, selling a home are also less viable.

Yet despite all the challenges, it remains rewarding work. People need our help as never before, and it feels good to be able to provide that help. And in looking to the future, I know that financial education is going to remain extremely important, and it will be satisfying to be part of providing that essential information.

Question and Answer Session

Question: Do you teach people how to correct errors in credit reports?

Stiller: Yes, we teach them how they can correct the incorrect information on their credit bureau report. It's not a large percentage of what we do. Most of the people who come to us do not have incorrect information, nor are they challenging their debts. They're just over their heads with debt and need a plan to get out.

But we do have some people who need to be taught what steps they can take to help improve their credit report, and we teach them that. We also have about 30 core education programs, a couple of which deal with this situation.

Question: What is the regulatory structure of the credit counseling industry?

Stiller: The credit counseling agencies are highly regulated now. The FDIC is looking at us, and the IRS is looking at us. Individual states have also passed all sorts of regulations.

Question: How do we keep the not-for-profits, who receive some of their funding from creditors, from responding to the incentive to put clients on a payment plan so that the creditors are made partially whole, rather than having the clients declare bankruptcy, which in many cases may be the smarter move?

Stiller: As I talked about earlier, the worst part of this job has been the inherent conflict of interest between lenders partially supporting credit counseling agencies and the fact that you're trying to give clients good, unbiased advice.

Having said that, first of all, you have to remember that creditor funding is the minority of funding. Second, there is a lot of regulatory scrutiny with the credit counseling industry, not just now but for years in the past, to make sure that doesn't happen. There is board scrutiny watching very closely to ensure that doesn't happen. Most of the boards now have no creditor representation or very little. There is staff scrutiny. You can't underestimate staff scrutiny. The staff members are being paid nonprofit wages; they're working for a social service agency because they want to help. If you just hinted that you did not give a consumer the very best advice, they would not only walk out the door but also go to the local newspaper. I'm very serious about that.

We also have ethical standards from our national association, the National Foundation for Credit Counseling, making it almost impossible to act against the consumer's interest. We also go through a rigorous accreditation process with the Council on Accreditation every four years, in the same way that universities do.

The biggest issue is recognizing that we have a potential conflict of interest. As I stated earlier, back in the 1970s, I went to my board and recommended that everybody who walks in the door get a factsheet on bankruptcy so that nobody could say we did not tell the consumer about bankruptcy. So, everyone who walks in the door gets information about bankruptcy, even if they're not in debt.

It is an important point about credit counseling agencies, but I truly don't think it's a problem. Nobody in the nonprofit world wants to hurt the consumer. The problem is with the for-profit models. That's where the disreputable agencies are.

Question: Do you have any data on whether the people who come to you ahead of time come back to you?

Stiller: There has been some research, but not enough. Certainly, anecdotally, there's hardly any recidivism, especially with the people who go on a Debt Management Plan. When they've learned to live on a strict budget for three or four years without credit and they know how freeing it can be to be out of debt after struggling for so long, the recidivism is very low.

On the education side, we need also to do a better job of looking at long-range behavior. Again, anecdotally, people tell us all the time about the difference that the education classes make. We have pre-tests and post-tests that always have good results.

What would really be good, and what is really needed, is to assess long-term behavioral change—follow people who are in education classes one year, two years, three years down the line. That's what we're trying to get to now.

Session 4: Saving and Investing by Low- and Middle-Income Households

The Two Worlds of Personal Finance: Implications for Promoting the Economic Well-Being of Low- and Moderate-Income Families

Robert I. Lerman
Institute Fellow in Labor and Social Policy
Urban Institute
Professor of Economics
American University

Eugene Steuerle
Institute Fellow and Richard B. Fisher Chair
Urban Institute

Robert Lerman

Two worlds of policy interest, research, and advocacy exist today: (1) mainstream finance, which relates best to the upper-income population, and (2) low-income personal finance, which relates best to the low- and middle-income population—a population, by the way, that extends even into the 50th percentile of income. The purpose of this presentation is to place in a broader context the key differences between these two worlds and then discuss the salient policy issues affecting the low- and middle-income world: human capital, housing and retirement savings, social insurance, and precautionary savings.

Mainstream and Low-to-Middle-Income Personal Finance. Mainstream finance concentrates on people who have high levels of income and financial assets. Although the life-cycle model can be applied to all levels of income and wealth, even that model emphasizes portfolio analysis and financial assets—and thus tends to ignore the realities of low- and middle-income households.

Mainstream personal finance also emphasizes the importance of income tax incentives for clients, such as the mortgage interest deduction. But for low-to-middle-income households, many such incentives are unlikely to apply. Such households have low marginal tax rates, and even when they do have positive rates, they rarely itemize. They live in a very different world from the population that best benefits from mainstream personal finance.

Beginning in the early 1990s, particularly with the publication of *Assets and the Poor*,[1] foundations began to show interest in the issue of low-income asset building. Actually, the term "asset building" is a bit of a misnomer. The real goal is sound balance sheets for low-income households.

■ *Initiatives for the low- and middle-income population.* Out of this new interest in the second world of finance, a few initiatives have arisen, each associated with a considerable amount of research.

The first initiative is embodied in individual development accounts (IDAs), which combine a financial literacy program with matched savings. To qualify for the program, individuals must have income below a certain level. The program provides financial education as well as encouragement to open a savings account. Participant savings in these accounts will be matched for approved purposes. For example, if a participant has saved $1,000 and the match is 3:1, that participant will actually have $4,000 to put toward an approved purpose, such as placing a down payment on a house, paying tuition, or starting a business.

Other important initiatives include (1) educating lower-income households about the importance of Social Security, which I will cover later in more detail; (2) spreading the word about the detrimental effects of high-cost alternative financial service products; and (3) liberalizing the often-misguided asset tests used in benefit programs. For example, to qualify for food stamps—a program used by approximately 25 million Americans (a dramatic increase as a result of the Great Recession)—individuals and households must pass a liquid assets test. In most states, people can own a home, even an expensive home, and still qualify for food stamps. But if they have too much money in a bank account, they will not qualify. Some housing programs have similarly misapplied asset tests, as does Temporary Assistance for Needy Families, a cash assistance program for the low-income population.

■ *Characteristics of low-income populations.* Large numbers of lower-income people are born to parents who are unmarried or who later divorce. They may be cohabiting, but such relationships tend to be less stable than marriages. The instability of the household can come from uncertainty about who is contributing

---

[1]Michael W. Sherraden, *Assets and the Poor: A New American Welfare Policy* (Armonk, NY: M.E. Sharpe, 1991).

to the household and who is spending the household's money. For low-income men, the buildup of arrearages in child support, often at high interest rates, is another issue that tends to be ignored in mainstream financial discussions.

Mainstream and low-income personal finance do, of course, have common elements, such as living within a budget, establishing good credit, and having retirement income. And the gradual recognition of the importance of behavioral economics plays a hand in both worlds. But each world has distinct perspectives on each of these elements, such as tax and transfer incentives, which I have already mentioned, and the importance of government social insurance, which Steuerle will cover, along with the policy debate centering on financial adequacy versus financial opportunity.

Human Capital. Human capital is the primary asset for most individuals, especially for low- and middle-income families, who have little in the way of financial assets, as **Figure 1** illustrates. In fact, Figure 1 significantly understates the potential of human capital because it is based on the earnings of 55-year-old workers, who it is assumed will retire in their early to mid-60s, which is not necessarily an accurate assumption for this population, as will be discussed later.

Figure 1. Estimated Human Capital and Total Assets for a 55-Year-Old Worker, Middle-Income Quintile

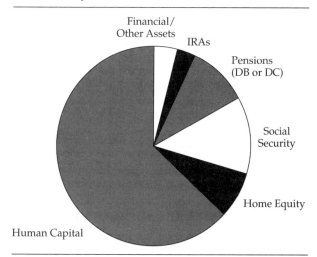

Notes: Human capital assumes an additional 19 years of work at the average Social Security wage. Working for an additional 19 years yields the same number of expected years spent in retirement as an average worker retiring in 1940.

Sources: Authors' estimates, with financial assets based upon Gordon Mermin, Sheila Zedlewski, and Desmond Toohey, "Diversity in Retirement Wealth Accumulation," Urban Institute Brief Series, no. 24 (December 2008). Estimates updated to 2010 dollars.

■ *Educational needs of the low-income population.* Consider also that mainstream financial advisers emphasize the importance of saving for college. Yet in low-income finance, this is hardly an issue. A top student from a low-income family is likely to get some scholarship support—perhaps a Federal Pell Grant—and most low-income students will go to state or community colleges that have low tuitions. Many Pell Grants will even pay living expenses, which will amply cover tuition and the other out-of-pocket costs of a community college.

Many individuals from low-income families will thrive and do well in college, which should continue to be encouraged. Yet when we talk about the development of human capital for this population, the bigger problem is the dropout rate for high school. The share of young people graduating from high school with a regular high school diploma has been relatively flat over the past few years, at approximately 75–78%. The graduation rate for more at-risk groups is around 60–62%. That statistic means 40% of these at-risk students are not earning a regular high school diploma, yet we focus the bulk of our effort on college. (Note that the high school dropout rate is somewhat disguised by the GED—an alternative high school credential—which has been shown to add little to human capital because the earning power of a person with a GED is little improved over the earning power of a high school dropout.)

■ *Regular employment and apprenticeships.* At low income levels, two factors are especially important. First is a steady work record. Work experience, even at low income levels, yields earnings gains over time, especially in a relatively stable occupational area. A stable work record is also essential to qualify for social insurance programs, such as unemployment insurance. Individuals with unstable work records often do not have enough quarters of prior employment to qualify for unemployment insurance. And a work record is essential for adequate coverage under the Social Security Old-Age, Survivors, and Disability Insurance (OASDI) program, which provides not just pension retirement but also survivor's insurance and disability insurance. Thus, the focus for human capital should be on improving the ability to earn.

Second, we need to develop better alternatives for career success aside from college. Many other countries have excellent apprenticeship programs in which people learn by doing. This idea is critical for the low- and middle-income population because with apprenticeship programs, participants are not forgoing earnings while they are building their human capital. While undergoing training, they typically earn a level of income similar to what they would at the beginning of a career, even as they gain the occupational skills that are so important for future earnings.

If I were to emphasize one policy message for the low- and middle-income population, it would be that we should help that population develop its human capital through steady earnings and expanded apprenticeship training.

Eugene Steuerle

As already mentioned, stocks and bonds rank fairly low in importance on the asset list for low- and middle-income families. Human capital is at the top of the list. After human capital come social security or social insurance (which we are presuming to count as an asset), homes, and then pension plans (both defined benefit and defined contribution). Only after all that do we come to the world of IRAs and portfolios of stocks and bonds.

Before addressing those asset groups, however, consider first the policy debate centering on financial adequacy versus financial opportunity for the low- and middle-income population.

Adequacy vs. Opportunity Policy Debate. The low-income advocacy community is divided between those who believe policy should focus on financial adequacy and those who think it is time to move in greater measure toward an opportunity agenda. My perspective is that as society expands its social welfare functions, the marginal returns from providing adequacy only become smaller and smaller. The natural progression, then, is to push more toward an opportunity agenda. But many advocates for low-income individuals either do not support an opportunity agenda or see it as an add-on because they cannot get something else.

For example, a number of groups, including the Ford Foundation, strongly advocate child accounts as a means of promoting saving and pushing into the opportunity agenda. But equally influential groups would rather stay with the adequacy agenda and simply use that money to increase SNAP (Supplemental Nutrition Assistance Program, formerly called food stamps). And this latter preference has a strong argument to support it. Promoting consumption at low income levels is easy to do. If I give low-income households an additional $100, they will more than likely spend the entire $100 on consumption. But if I help them invest in education or child accounts with matched funds, success is variable. The risk of failure is much higher. They may not study in the case of education or hang onto the saving in the case of subsidies for deposits to saving accounts.

One could also argue that the opportunity agenda is more regressive, that the ambitious person—the person more committed to long-term goals—will gain more from the opportunity agenda than those who are less committed. *Ex post*, then, the opportunity agenda will sometimes favor those who end up with higher incomes, such as those who take advantage of the educational subsidies.

But the "grand compromise" that now exists between liberals and conservatives tends to provide the most opportunity subsidies to those with higher incomes and then to the middle-income population. The opportunity subsidies provided to low-income households tend to be small and in some programs, nonexistent. There are exceptions, as in the case of subsidies for education.

Even there, however, the higher-income group still often gets more than the lower income group because more of the former take advantage of these subsidies, including state support for public colleges.

Thus, opportunity subsidies tend to go to higher-income people, and adequacy subsidies—the consumption subsidies—go to low-income people. Together, this mix of policies distorts incentives in ways that discourage low-income populations from trying to raise themselves to middle-class status.

Housing and Retirement Savings. From the early 1990s through the early 2000s, 25- to 35-year-olds from middle-wealth populations were saving $7,000 to $8,000 per year, as shown in **Figure 2**. People who were 35–45 years old were saving about $12,000, and people 45–55 years old were saving about $18,000 annually. With all the talk about the low savings rate in the United States, these amounts might seem implausible. How did middle-income families making only $50,000 a year save this much money? They did so through Social Security wealth, homeownership, and retirement savings. The growth of the last two depends on behaviors that become routine and lead to returns that also compound year after year.

If we wish to increase saving by households, the behaviors that we should all be emphasizing include paying off the mortgage and putting money into a retirement account. We don't just need to stick to traditional methods. For instance, one initiative to encourage homeownership would be to make it easier for some to convert their rental subsidies into homeownership at low cost.

Note also that the importance of other financial assets, such as savings accounts, is relatively small. For many people, no matter their income level, most of their wealth is in their home and their retirement account. Certainly this is true at low income levels, even among those with only a high school diploma or less. Bottom line: Housing and retirement accounts are where most households save.

Importance of Social Insurance. When it comes to retirement, Social Security and Medicare, in the United States, provide the most important assets not only for low- and middle-income families but also for upper-middle-income families. I have estimated that the lifetime value of Social Security and Medicare (including a rough estimate for the value of backup Medicaid if a person ends up in a nursing home for a long time) is now close to $1 million per couple. That value is in excess of all the private wealth for about 75% or 80% of the population.

For the vast majority of people, their most important portfolio decisions relate to these social insurance policies. Whether or not these programs are sustainable at that level as the nation advances into the future is another question, but right now, that is where the money is. Decisions related to social insurance

Figure 2. Annual Wealth Accrual per Adult between Early 1990s and Early 2000s for Typical Households

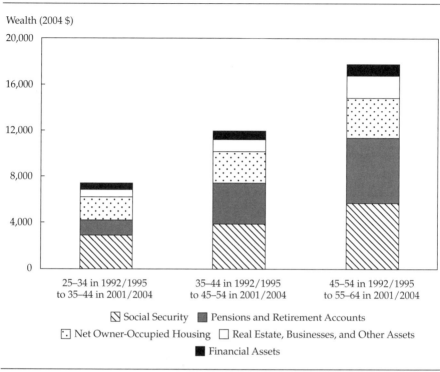

Sources: Urban Institute calculations from the 1992, 1995, 2001, and 2004 Surveys of Consumer Finances and the Dynamic Simulation of Income Model (DYNASIM3).

are even more important for low-income individuals because their replacement rates (the portion of pre-retirement or pre-disability income replaced by social insurance) are even higher than they are for higher-income people.

Figure 3 offers another view of this asset allocation (excluding the human capital component and Medicare) for both the low-income and the middle-income populations. Both charts again demonstrate the dominance of Social Security and homeownership, which account for 77% of low-income assets (51% + 26%) and 54% of middle-income assets (34% + 20%).

Combining these various figures, we conclude that the most important portfolio decision that the majority of low- and middle-income individuals make is when to retire (or from the other perspective, how long to keep working). It is a far more important decision than the choice of the best allocation of stocks and bonds in a portfolio. According to our research at the Urban Institute, for every additional year worked, annual income increases thereafter—in real, inflation-adjusted terms—by about 8%, largely because of the way

Figure 3. Composition of Assets for a Worker, Bottom- and Middle-Income Quintile, Aged 55–64 (2010 dollars)

A. Bottom Income Quintile, Total = $177,600

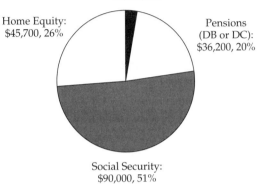

Financial/Other Assets: $5,700, 3%

Home Equity: $45,700, 26%

Pensions (DB or DC): $36,200, 20%

Social Security: $90,000, 51%

B. Middle Income Quintile, Total = $390,600

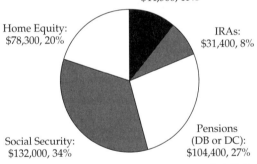

Financial/Other Assets: $44,500, 11%

Home Equity: $78,300, 20%

IRAs: $31,400, 8%

Social Security: $132,000, 34%

Pensions (DB or DC): $104,400, 27%

Notes: Financial and other assets include bank accounts, certificates of deposit (CDs), stocks, bonds, mutual funds, property, businesses, vehicles, and other financial assets net of nonhousing debt. Social Security and defined-benefit (DB) pension wealth are the expected present value of future benefits. Future Social Security benefits are based on lifetime earnings records that were statistically matched to adults in the Survey of Consumer Finance (SCF) from the Dynamic Simulation of Income Model (DYNASIM3). Future DB pension benefits are based on expected or current benefits. Analysis combines the 2001 and 2004 surveys. All amounts are in 2004 dollars.
Source: Gordon Mermin, Sheila Zedlewski, and Desmond Toohey, "Diversity in Retirement Wealth Accumulation," Urban Institute Brief Series, no. 24 (December 2008). Estimates updated to 2010 dollars.

that Social Security is designed. All Social Security old-age benefits are paid out as an annuity. One "buys" additional annuity income by forgoing receipt of Social Security at an earlier age (say, 62), thus increasing the size of the annuitized payout at the later age (say, 70).

The average person retiring at 62 has a life expectancy of 20–30 years. If people can increase their annual retirement income by 8% just by working one additional year, they accrue a lot of financial protection. If they work eight additional years, shifting their retirement age from 62 to 70, they can typically increase their retirement income by two-thirds or more, which is a lot more than they can obtain through any other portfolio decision.

Figure 4 shows just how far we have come in providing years of support since Social Security was started in the United States. In 1940, a few years after the system was first created, the average person retired at age 68, with 65 being the earliest retirement age allowed. If we assume retirement lasts the same number of years now as in 1940, the age at retirement today would be 75 because of increasing life expectancies. Go 60 years into the future to 2070, and the

Figure 4. Age of Retirement If Number of Years of Benefits Remains Constant

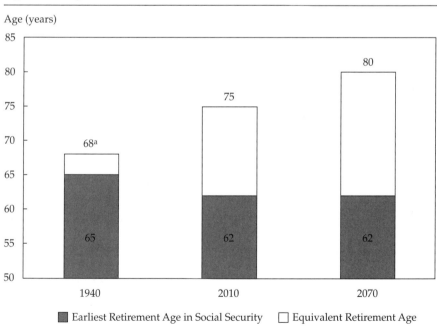

Age (years)

ᵃAverage retirement age in 1940 and 1950.
Source: Eugene C. Steuerle and Stephanie Rennane, "Social Security and the Budget," Urban Institute, Retirement Policy Program Policy Brief No. 28 (2010).

equivalent retirement age rises to 80. But we have not raised the normal Social Security retirement age significantly, and people are living in retirement for 10 or more years longer than they did when Social Security was first created.

Soon we will have a system in which the adult population is scheduled to be on Social Security for about one-third of its adult life. Given current birth rates, which are about at replacement, that means also that soon about one-third of the adult population in the United States will be on the system. Imagine people having to save enough over two-thirds of their adult lives to support themselves for the final one-third. To do this using private savings, one would have to save about a third of one's income every year. We're not even saving close to a fraction of this amount. Thus, the principal issues regarding retirement for most people are deciding how long to continue working and how to manage their Social Security.

Precautionary Savings. Although certain advocacy groups, such as the Ford Foundation, are encouraging child savings accounts and matched savings for individual development accounts (IDAs), these are not the areas where people will see high rates of return. One could argue, in fact, that many such savings accounts are earning negative real rates of return right now. Yet such accounts are still an extremely important vehicle for precautionary savings, not only for the money accrued and the safety net they provide but also for the positive effect they have on individuals' money management skills and credit profiles.

Many low-income individuals have low credit scores, and these low scores make it difficult for such individuals to obtain low-cost, short-term credit, which they often need because of their lack of liquid savings. They thus turn to high-cost vehicles, such as RALs and RACs (refund anticipation loans and refund anticipation checks, respectively), which can pay them their earned income credits or tax refunds as much as two weeks sooner than payment would be made by the IRS. But RALs and RACs typically cost $50 or $65.

A recent study by the Urban Institute using more than 1 million IRS returns found that, among other things, participants who received $1 or more in interest from a savings vehicle, such as a bank account, were five times less likely to make use of RALs and RACs. This finding has, of course, a simultaneity problem because it does not prove that being "banked" led participants to be more precautionary or make better use of their funds and thus avoid high-cost vehicles, but it is a finding worth taking seriously. Low-income households who open savings accounts, who engage with the financial sector in the right way and thus experience compounding and real returns on assets, become better managers of their finances. That outcome is valuable, even when the returns on savings accounts are as low as they are today.

Annuitizing Social Security. As I mentioned earlier, the Social Security annuity is one of the best deals on the market. Almost no one knows it, and no one gets good advice on it. More often than not, people are advised to "take your money now." When people look at their Social Security account statements, they see that the Social Security Administration essentially is saying that it is almost immaterial whether they take their money now or later. The actual statement refers to a form of "actuarial neutrality" between taking one's money now or later. But those are not risk-adjusted statements. Once account risk is considered, the choice is not actuarially neutral. I challenge anyone to find a better deal than Social Security, which is, in essence, an inflation-indexed annuity that pays about 8 cents on the dollar year after year with the full protection of the U.S. government.

Most people assume that the decision to retire, the decision to take Social Security, and the decision to buy an annuity within Social Security are one and the same decision. In truth, they are three separable decisions. First, people can retire and not take their Social Security, which means that the amount of annuity they eventually take, especially after age 66, is technically up to them. After age 66, participants are eligible to receive a delayed retirement credit of $8 for every $100 of benefit not taken. Technically, retirees could take their benefits for six months, then not take them for six months, then take the benefits again for six months, and then again not take them for the next six months. Essentially, they can convert half of their Social Security checks for those two years into an annuity—effectively achieving half retirement for that period. If such a strategy is technically possible, why not let people choose it up front? Why not give them the option, perhaps up to the size of their Social Security check, to buy a Social Security annuity up front? A retirement planner might then advise them to put aside $100,000 into the Social Security annuity and withdraw from their 401(k), just as if they were buying a private annuity.

The Social Security benefit is not currently described as I have suggested, but there is no technical reason why people should not build up their annuity protection by taking Social Security benefits optimally. Furthermore, such a strategy does not have to cost Social Security any money. It is neither a liberal nor a conservative position.

Conclusion. Keep in mind four key policy issues. First, human capital is by far the most important asset for the majority of the population—even for people in their 50s and often into their early 60s. That people work and then suddenly hit a point when they must retire entirely because they have moved from being fully productive to unproductive is an outmoded and silly stereotype and assumption about their capacity.

Second, Social Security benefits are the most important nonhuman capital asset for low- and middle-income families, and a stable employment record is essential for realizing these benefits to their fullest.

Third, homeownership and pensions are other key mechanisms for achieving middle-class wealth. But the lessons learned from saving and experiencing the value not only of compounded savings but also of the positive effect that saving can have on credit scores are crucial to long-term improvement. This is an important area of emphasis for behavioral economics and finance education initiatives.

Finally, the tax and financial incentives currently available to low- and middle-income families should be reconsidered and reallocated in a way that helps low-income families progress onto a path that leads to middle-class status. Programs to promote opportunity should extend to all.

Session 4: Saving and Investing by Low- and Middle-Income Households

Discussion

Laurence Kotlikoff, Moderator
William Fairfield Warren Professor
Boston University

Moshe A. Milevsky
Associate Professor of Finance
York University, Toronto
Executive Director, The IFID Centre

Moshe A. Milevsky

According to Lerman and Steuerle, financial economists and their research tend to go where the money is. I will be the first to plead guilty to that. I find it more appealing to teach my students about asset allocation, the best way to use hedge funds, and whether to buy puts to protect the portfolio than to discuss individual development accounts for lower-income families. But during the course of my presentation, I will suggest some ideas for shifting the interest to low- and middle-income households.

Financial Sophistication of the Very Poor. In 2009, Princeton University Press published *Portfolios of the Poor: How the World's Poor Live on $2 a Day*.[1] The authors spent a year living among and observing very low-income individuals in emerging economies, such as Nepal, South Africa, and India. The authors asked these individuals, who were literally living on US$2 a day, to keep journals and track how they managed their money.

After interviewing the participants and examining the journals, the authors concluded that low-income people are actually extremely sophisticated in their management of personal finances. According to the *Economist*, these individuals do

> what economists like to call consumption smoothing; spreading spending out
> in a way that ensures that what you eat one day is not determined by what you

---

[1]Daryl Collins, Jonathan Morduch, Stuart Rutherford, and Orlanda Ruthven, *Portfolios of the Poor: How the World's Poor Live on $2 a Day* (Princeton, NJ: Princeton University Press, 2009).

have earned that day or the day before. The subjects used a combination of loans and savings to ensure that their lives were not, literally, hostage to fortune. Hardly anyone lived utterly hand to mouth. The research provides evidence of the sophistication with which poor people think about their finances.[2]

In those weeks or days in which they had higher income than expected—for example, they earned $2.50 as opposed to $2—they would save the 50 cents because they knew that there would be periods of time when they would earn less than $2. They entered into agreements with other community members whereby they would share the assets they accrued during good days so that they would have a subsidy during bad days.

Economists can learn a lot about consumption smoothing from low- and middle-income households.

Importance of Human Capital. I agree with Lerman and Steuerle's emphasis on the value of human capital, especially early in life and especially among low- and middle-income (or LMI) individuals. When people are in their 20s, the most valuable asset class they possess is human capital, as **Figure 1** shows. This human capital can be calculated as the present value of the wages a person will earn until retirement. Unfortunately, it is hard to

Figure 1.   Life Cycle of the Personal Balance Sheet

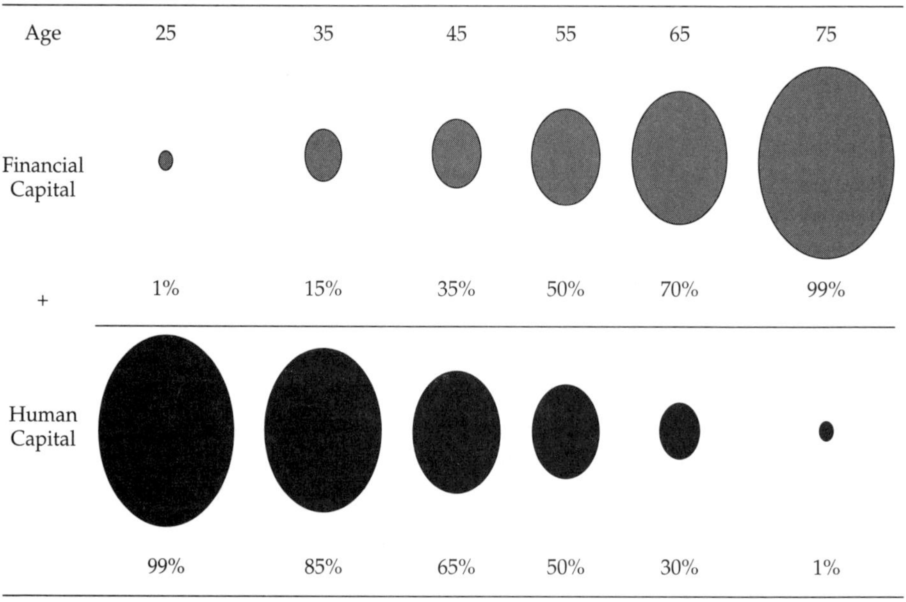

Age	25	35	45	55	65	75
Financial Capital	1%	15%	35%	50%	70%	99%
Human Capital	99%	85%	65%	50%	30%	1%

[2]"Smooth Operators," *Economist* (16 May 2009):82 (http://www.economist.com/node/13665319).

convince many people that human capital should be placed on a balance sheet and treated as an asset. Young adults do not see the point, and accountants insist it is not sound accounting.

One of my esteemed colleagues at the business school, who is also on the board of the Canadian accounting standards board, said to me recently, "Moshe, you cannot capitalize future earnings. Once you earn it, it is yours, but to discount 30 years of wages and put it on the balance sheet? You cannot treat that as an asset." My response to him was, "You are in your 60s. You are about to retire. You have done well for yourself and have quite a bit of financial capital but not much human capital. How much of your financial capital would you be willing to give up today to turn back the clock to make you 25 again and get your human capital back?" This response caused him to pause.

Not long ago, I asked a group of retirees in Florida, "How many of you would be willing to cut a check for half of your financial capital to make you 35 years younger and give you your human capital back?" Not only did all of the hands go up, but also a lady in the back screamed, "All of it! Take all of it, and make me 20 again!" Yet when I ask undergraduates or MBA students who are in their early to mid-20s the same question, it does not resonate. They do not see the value of their own human capital. All they see is their debt and their minuscule financial capital.

Nevertheless, at some point in our lives, we realize how valuable human capital is and how much money we are willing to give up in order to get that human capital. So, why not start valuing it from Day 1? Put a number on it and start treating it like an asset class. We do this by figuring out its risk–return characteristics and how it correlates with financial capital. People should be encouraged to invest in human capital and create more of it.

Investing in Human Capital: Evidence from Canada. All children in Canada below the age of 18 whose parents have enrolled them in a Registered Education Savings Plan (RESP) are also eligible to participate in the Canada Education Savings Grant (CESG) program, which has at its core an appreciation of the importance of investing in human capital. Here is how it works: Anyone who is born to an LMI family (annual income of less than C\$41,000) and is properly enrolled will immediately receive a \$500 grant (or bond) to be invested in an RESP, which is a tax-sheltered investment account similar to a Roth IRA through which participants can pick the investment types they prefer.

Moreover, parents are allowed to add to this account every year, and for every dollar contributed by the family, a match of 40% is provided, up to \$500 annually. Above the first \$500, a 20% grant is provided for the next \$2,000 of annual contributions. Even high-income families (i.e., those with more than \$41,000 in annual income) can receive a 20% grant on the first \$2,500 of contributions.

For example, assume that an LMI family manages to save and contribute $750 a year to their child's RESP. For that, the family will receive a grant of $250 (that is, 40% of the first $500 plus 20% of the remainder). Thus, their $750 investment immediately becomes a $1,000 investment. When the children enroll in college, they can start withdrawing the money at their marginal tax rate (which is likely to be close to zero), although the parents remain the trustees.

Now assume that an LMI family has contributed $12,000 over the course of 16 years and that the money has earned a steady 5% return each year. When all the grants are included, the compound annual return is equivalent to 9.12%, and thus the family has $25,000 in an account that can be withdrawn by the child with little or no tax due. Basically, this is a very good deal. And yet a study conducted by Statistics Canada found that of the entire population of families who are saving money for their children's education, 69.3% are participating in the CESG program. Of those surveyed families earning less than $50,000 annually, only 56% are using the CESG program. If a parent has less than a high school education, the percentage drops to 49.5%. Curiously, if the child is female, the percentage of families using the program is 71.2% but if the child is male, it drops to 67.4%.

These statistics mean, unfortunately, that the people who most need the program—those with low or middle incomes and those with lower levels of education—are least likely to use it. But even among those who understand the value of investing in human capital and who have dedicated money for education, the take-up rate is relatively low.

Avenues for Research. To frame a discussion about how LMI households might differ from the rest of the population and thus suggest some fertile areas for research, I consider first the standard utility maximization framework, the life-cycle model, which is

$$V^* = \max_{c_t} \int_0^D e^{-\rho t} \left({}_t P x \right) u\left(c_t\right) dt, \tag{1}$$

where ρ is the subjective discount rate, $({}_t P_x)$ is the survival probability, and c_t is the consumption function subject to the (dynamic) constraint:

$$\dot{F}_t = v\left(F_t\right) F_t + w_t - c_t, \tag{2}$$

where F_t is the trajectory of wealth, w_t is the wage (or pension) process, and

$$v\left(F_t\right) = \begin{cases} v, & F_t > 0 \\ \hat{v}, & F_t \le 0 \end{cases}. \tag{3}$$

■ *Applying the life-cycle model to LMI households.* To determine the alloca-tion of an individual's wealth over time, the following factors are involved:

- the amount to save and amount to consume,

- the probability of survival, and

- the evolution of wealth over time.

This is a deterministic model in which everyone invests his or her money in the safest asset possible. Therefore, no uncertainty exists, which is not realistic. Nonetheless, a life-cycle model framework still offers much worth considering.

The life cycle of an LMI household differs from that of higher-income households in several ways. First, it has lower levels of wealth (F_0) and a high wage-to-wealth ratio (w_t/F_t). The amount of income brought in versus the amount saved is very high. Second, the subjective probability of survival ($_tp_x$) is much lower on average for LMI individuals, which may negate the advantage of deferring social security benefits, which under normal circumstances can lead to an 8% higher rate of return per year of deferral. When conducting an LMI life-cycle analysis, the survival probability should be tilted downward.

Third, the marginal tax rate function tends to be extremely steep. We see this in Canada, and I presume it happens in the United States as well. At some of the lower to middle income levels, a bump upward of $10,000 in income can move a household from a 20% marginal tax rate to about a 45% rate. But at about $150,000 of income, the rate flattens out at about 48% and remains essentially constant at any income beyond that. Simply moving up or down in the lower income brackets introduces decisions about when to take income. Should I take it this year, or is it worthwhile to wait? What does this mean in terms of life-cycle utility?

Finally, the LMI population experiences a much greater asymmetry in interest rates than other income populations. The borrowing rate tends to be much higher than the lending (or investment) rate.

■ *Potential research questions.* The following are possible areas of research on LMI households from a normative life-cycle point of view.

- Should LMI households be encouraged to annuitize additional wealth at retirement? It seems to be accepted wisdom that putting more into annui-ties is better than putting less into annuities. But that is not necessarily the case when the mortality rate is high, which makes the cost of annuities also high. Investors have to be extremely longevity-risk averse to buy an annu-ity priced as though they were going to live 15 years longer than they are likely to. If tontines were available and the investors could renegotiate the tontine every instant, then yes, they would likely take the premium over the market. But if investors with a very low level of longevity-risk aversion are asked to buy an annuity that is locked in for the rest of their lives, the result might be different.

- Should LMI individuals wait until age 70 to withdraw money from their tax-sheltered accounts (such as IRAs), or should they withdraw their money earlier? When the marginal effective tax rate is very steep, it might make sense to pull it out earlier.

- Should LMI households purchase term or whole life insurance? The typical wisdom is that individuals should buy term and invest the difference. But whole life insurance policies have optionality built in; policyholders can scale up their policies, which can be valuable with volatile mortality rates. Mortality rates are stochastic, so the optionality of whole life might make sense for LMI households.

- Should we dissuade LMI seniors from borrowing money? This seems like an especially important issue when so many LMI seniors have only social security and the equity in their homes, particularly considering that such equity is difficult to access.

Retirement May Not Be a Choice. Some interesting evidence found by Statistics Canada goes directly to the issue of delaying social security for as long as possible. (As in the United States, the longer Canadians delay collecting Old Age Security benefits, the greater the investment return.)

When Statistics Canada asked people from the general population why they retired, the following were among the responses they received. (Participants were allowed to choose more than one response, so the amounts add up to more than 100%.)

Financially possible	34%
Wanted to stop work	33
Completed required years	29
Health and disability	24
Caregiving	7

Note particularly the health and disability response. A quarter of the responding population retired because they could not work anymore. They might very well have wanted to stay in the labor force, but physically they could no longer do the work. So, the optimal time to retire may not apply to a quarter of the population because delaying retirement may simply not be an option. This is a reality we need to keep in mind.

Concluding Thoughts. I agree with the main premise. Most financial economists who work in normative life-cycle modeling ought to spend more time thinking about the model's application to LMI households. As we have seen, the extremely poor households are quite capable of sophisticated consumption smoothing. The non-extreme households are less sophisticated in this regard.

However, even if we do model relevant problems for LMI households, we then have to locate the right audience and communicate our findings to them. And even if we do these things, we cannot guarantee that LMI households will adopt the advice we provide. We can advise LMI households to take advantage of the immediate return of 40% provided by the CESG, but will anybody listen? And that leads to another possible reason for the kind of research typically done by most financial economists: They are not going where the money *is* but where the money *listens*.

Question and Answer Session

Question: If the income ceiling in your study were less than $30,000, would the participation rate be materially affected?

Milevsky: Although Statistics Canada did not share the data for every income level, it did break them down to those earning $30,000 of income and less. The participation rate for that group was about 45%, as compared with 56.2% for those earning $50,000 and less. In contrast, above $100,000 of income, the participation rate was 95%. Those households received only 20% instead of 40%, and at some point, it is scaled down to about 10%. But it demonstrates that those higher earners were aware and took advantage of the program.

Question: How can the grant money be used?

Milevsky: The rules are very liberal. It started as just tuition, then it included books, then dormitory costs, then anything that was an apprenticeship. As long as you can prove it is for education, you can pull the funds out.

Question: What country is best at offering apprenticeship programs?

Lerman: The Swiss program is probably the most effective. It is also the one best suited to the United States because the Swiss have a flexible labor market system. Despite the fact that only about 45% of the apprentices stay with a firm after their training, the evidence indicates that most of the firms recover the costs during the apprenticeship period itself because the apprentices are producing in a way that allows them to substitute for highly skilled workers who would be highly compensated. Switzerland also has a high-quality university sector, but not everybody needs to go to a university to get a good job and have a good career.

Germany also has a very good system. If individuals pass a certain exam, they can go to college for such a small charge that, compared with U.S. standards, the cost approximates zero. Of the people who take and pass the exam, perhaps one-quarter first go into an apprenticeship, which indicates that apprenticeship training is not a dead end.

Many people like to learn by doing and thus experience a sense of pride and accomplishment when they complete a high-standard apprenticeship program. Many of them go on to college or university. We have a lot to learn from countries that provide such programs, especially if we want to enhance the earning power and incentives of people in the LMI range. Today, we have huge gaps between young men and young women in completing college and even high school. It's a huge problem, and I think we need to take it seriously. I am not against college. I just think, as in so many other areas of financial planning, we need to diversify the routes to career success.

Question: According to a financial capability study done by FINRA in 2011, half of the population does not have three months of income as precautionary savings. How can we advise people to keep their wealth in illiquid assets, such as a house or a retirement savings account, when they have not yet learned to address their short-term issues?

Steuerle: Lerman and I discuss the usefulness of precautionary savings in our paper. But to summarize, we take averages, which tend to stereotype. The low-income population is an extremely diverse group of people with a variety of needs, capabilities, and life expectancies.

Precautionary savings is extremely important and often the place to start building for the long term. By building up a little precautionary savings, households learn how important even a little bit of money can be, and that understanding is often the first step toward homeownership and retirement savings.

In fact, one way of building up precautionary savings is by using the right type of retirement account. Borrowing against employee savings is not necessarily a bad way to structure some precautionary savings. Another means, which Lerman mentioned, is the automobile. As an auto loan is paid off, the automobile becomes an asset rather than just a debt.

Comment: Precautionary savings is also critical to maintaining a good credit score. We asked people in six low-income areas what interest rate they were paying on their mortgages. We found that they could have saved 25–30% had they been able to get prime-type mortgages. So, the link to precautionary savings is vital. If individuals can pay their bills and accrue some precautionary savings, they can maintain a good credit record.

Question: Do you address the three milestone events—having a child, getting married, and graduating from high school—when discussing LMI populations?

Steuerle: It was not emphasized in this paper, but Lerman has worked extensively on those very aspects. He was the one who originally came up with the statistic that if families of all income levels had the same rate of marriage, much of the racial and other differences in poverty rates could be explained away.

My own work has stressed the hundreds of billions of dollars of marriage penalties throughout our tax and welfare systems. We could talk about that in terms of its potential social impact as well. Such distortions occur because of the huge marginal tax rates caused by the loss of benefits as income increases (e.g., the decline in the value of the earned income tax credit or the loss of Medicaid). So yes, we've worked on some of those issues, but I wouldn't say we have yet integrated them into a milestone analysis.

Question: Do you have any suggestions for providing institutional support for encouraging people to keep their skills up-to-date?

Comment: Aside from formal apprenticeships, a considerable amount of training takes place at work sites. Even in middle-career years, a lot of firm-based training occurs. Most of the research indicates that employer-led training has a very good return associated with it, especially for the worker but also for the firms themselves.

When firms report their profits, they expense the amounts spent on training. Yet even though businesses often say that their people are their most important asset, they do not record training expenses as an asset or an enhancement of that asset (or income) partly because, in an accounting sense, they don't fully own that asset.

I think the accounting profession still ought to find a way to recognize the enhancement of a firm's workforce capabilities. Doing so might provide greater recognition of the value of training and have the systemic effect of increasing the amount of employer-led training. That change would play a big role in helping to raise skill levels.

Question: If, as you indicated, 24% of the general Canadian population retired because they were not physically able to work any longer, I imagine the percentage would be even higher for the LMI population. Wouldn't this strengthen the argument for Steuerle's proposal to let people take their Social Security early and use a portion of it to buy a future deferred annuity?

Steuerle: My annuity comment was directed more at middle-income rather than low-income earners. However, for the many members of the low-income population that may survive a long time, the Social Security annuity is a very good deal. In fact, if individuals can work another year, the biggest percentage increase in post-retirement income is with lower incomes. One year's extra earnings for a low-income earner is usually a bigger proportion of overall income. The well-to-do have more income from financial assets, whereas the low-income population, by being more dependent upon earnings, usually get the biggest proportionate gains on total income by working longer.

For example, a low-income earner without savings may work an extra year and have her Social Security income—and, hence, total income—rise by 8% in later years. A richer person with savings may see Social Security income also rise by 8%, but total income by, say, only 5%.

Session 5: Financial Education: What Have We Learned So Far?

School-Based Financial Education: Not Ready for Prime Time

Lewis Mandell
Senior Fellow
Aspen Institute Initiative on Financial Security

Introduction

A great deal of research has shown that many Americans make expensive "mistakes" in their personal financial decisions (Campbell 2006). Because those with the fewest financial resources are most likely to make such mistakes, standards of living become even more poorly distributed (Lusardi and Mitchell 2006; Mandell 2009a).

Although financial education might be the logical antidote to these mistakes, successful implementation of such educational programs has not occurred. There is the belief in many states that future financial mistakes could be prevented by forcing all students to take a high school course in personal finance.

Educational Mandates

Because it is so difficult to educate adults when they need financial education to make critical decisions, many people have decided that personal finance should become part of the basic education of all students. This suggested mandate was made by the National Association of State Boards of Education (NASB 2006) and was reiterated by the report of the President's Advisory Council on Financial Literacy (U.S. Department of the Treasury 2008), whose first recommendation is to "mandate financial education in all schools for students in grades Kindergarten through 12" (p. 3).

Most mandated instruction in personal finance appears to be at the high school level. There are two rationales for this. One is that students completing high school are on the verge of adulthood and will soon be making important financial decisions relating to student loans, credit cards, and auto insurance. Of equal importance is the fact that high school is the last opportunity society has to mandate required education for students. Few college-age students opt to take courses in personal finance, even when they are available, and many students do not attend college at all. In his OECD report, Mundy (2009) suggests that the subject is not more commonly chosen as a useful elective because many students see it as being mathematically complex. Mandell (2009b) finds that such courses are not effective in promoting financial literacy and even less effective than classes in high school in promoting self-beneficial financial behavior.

Opponents of such mandates fear the implementation costs to strapped local governments and downsized faculties, while others demand evidence that such courses would be effective. In spite of these objections, mandated courses in personal finance appear to be politically popular. A 2009 Council for Economic Education survey found that 15 states required personal finance to be offered by all high schools and 13 required students to take such a course as a requirement for graduation, more than double the number of states with such requirements in 2004 (Council for Economic Education 2009).

Effectiveness of Personal Financial Education

The effectiveness of personal finance education in improving personal financial knowledge has been seriously challenged. The Jump$tart Coalition for Personal Financial Literacy has run large-scale, national, pencil-and-paper surveys of high school seniors every other year since the 1997–98 academic year to measure financial literacy. Nearly 23,000 students have participated in the six surveys. Beginning with the 2000 survey, students were asked about their education relating to personal finance. Every one of the five surveys beginning in 2000 found that taking a full-semester high school class devoted to personal finance or money management has not been shown to have a significant positive impact on financial literacy scores.

This seriously questions the usefulness of mandating the teaching of financial literacy. Willis (2008) cites the Jump$tart findings in her paper "Against Financial-Literacy Education" and concludes that "the search for effective financial literacy education should be replaced by a search for policies more conducive to good consumer financial outcomes" (p. 198).

In addition to Professor Willis, some behavioral economists argue that information-based financial education is likely to have, at best, a modest impact (for recent reviews, see de Meza, Irlenbusch, and Reyniers 2008; De Mello Ferreira 2010; and Yoong 2010). Some economists feel that consumers would be better protected by a reversion to a limited number of simple "plain vanilla" financial products similar to those that existed prior to the elimination of Regulation Q. These may include a single home mortgage (i.e., 30 year, fixed rate, 20% down, no pre-payment penalty) and a mandated 401(k) plan with a pre-determined asset allocation based on age. Although the Dodd–Frank financial reform bill of 2010, which was signed into law by President Obama, appeared to reject the mandating of plain vanilla products, recent Fed proposals that have been put out for comment propose granting banks that offer very simple, fixed-rate, low-fee mortgages "safe harbor" protection from legal claims that loans were unfair or deceptive, thereby bringing plain vanilla mortgages in through the back door.

A Review of the Evidence Relating to Financial Literacy

Several surveys since the mid-1990s have shown that American youth and adults lack the basic knowledge needed to make self-beneficial financial choices (see Chen and Volpe 1998 and Volpe, Chen, and Liu 2006 for a review). Using the most recent wave of the 1997 National Longitudinal Survey of Youth, Lusardi, Mitchell, and Curto (2010) confirm the low levels of financial literacy of young adults. They find that fewer than one-third possessed a basic understanding of interest rates, inflation, and risk diversification.

Young adults who lack basic financial literacy have been shown to have poor financial decision-making ability as well as increased levels of debt (Norvilitis, Merwin, Osberg, Roehling, Young, and Kamas 2006). Sallie Mae (2009) found that median credit card debt among college students increased by 74% from 2004 to 2008. More than 50% of students surveyed by the Public Interest Research Group Education Fund (PIRG) (2008) reported that they used credit cards to finance day-to-day expenses, including textbooks and tuition.[1] This may be due to the fact that many young adults do not understand the long-term consequences of sizeable debt accumulation or the effect of poor credit decisions on their credit scores (Seaward and Kemp 2000; Roberts and Jones 2001; Norvilitis, Szablicki, and Wilson 2003).

Somewhat earlier, Danes and Hira (1987) found a relationship between young adults' financial behavior and their future earning capacity. Non-self-beneficial financial habits developed while young, combined with limited understanding of money management, could endure into the future (Hira 2002).

The inability to make sound financial decisions often persists throughout life, implying that many older adults do not learn from their mistakes. Lusardi and Mitchell (2006) used the 2004 U.S. Health and Retirement Study (HRS) to ascertain the basic financial knowledge of those over the age of 50. Their questions, testing an understanding of interest compounding, the effects of

---

[1] This may become less of a problem in the United States because credit card regulations implemented in 2010 ban card issuers from providing credit cards to people under age 21 unless co-signed by an adult or unless the applicant can show an independent source of income.

inflation, and risk diversification, found that financial illiteracy is widespread among these older adults and is particularly severe among women, the elderly, and those with less education.

Financial illiteracy is common in many other developed countries, including those in Europe as well as Australia, Japan, and Korea (OECD 2005). Using micro data from European countries (similar to the HRS data in the United States), Christelis, Jappelli, and Padula (2010) find that most respondents in Europe have low scores on financial literacy scales.

Hypotheses Regarding the Ineffectiveness of High School Classes

A number of hypotheses have been advanced to explain why high school classes in financial management or personal finance are ineffective in raising levels of financial literacy. One was that students who opted to take such classes were less likely to be academically talented and college-bound. Mandell (2002) disproved this hypothesis by showing that no differences exist in the proportions of college-bound and non-college-bound students taking such a class.

A second hypothesis for the poor educational outcomes was that high school teachers of personal finance were not very well trained to teach in this area. However, Mandell (2004) found just the opposite, that those who taught full-time courses in money management or personal finance tended to be well educated in the area and experienced. In fact, more than 90% of schools used the same teachers to teach these full-semester courses year after year, of whom two-thirds had a graduate degree in business, consumer economics, or related fields and nearly all of whom had at least an undergraduate degree in the appropriate field.

Of genuine surprise was the finding from the 2008 survey (Mandell 2008b) that high school classes in personal finance were not targeted at seniors who had the most to gain from them, and presumably the greatest motivation to learn the material. Rather, nearly half the students who took a course in personal finance or money management were freshmen, sophomores, and juniors.[2]

Success of Stock Market Games

Playing a stock market game is the only school-based educational program consistently related to higher financial literacy scores. Starting with the 2000 Jump$tart survey, when it was first measured, students who played a stock market game in class did 3 to 4 percentage points better than all students.[3] Playing such an interactive game appears to stimulate general interest in (and possibly a positive attitude toward) personal finance. Students who played a stock market game in class tended to do better than others, not just in questions relating

---

[2]Actually, sophomores and juniors learned more in the classes than did seniors.
[3]On a mean score base at about 50%, this translates to a 6–8% increase in financial literacy.

to investments but also in every subject category. And, as we will see below, they consistently did better than the other students in all five surveys, on 16 of the 31 test questions, in spite of the fact that they did not differ demographically from the other students.

Financial Literacy and Financial Behavior

Several studies have found that financial literacy is positively related to self-beneficial financial behavior. In a well-known study, Hilgert, Hogarth, and Beverly (2003) formed a "Financial Practices Index" based upon self-beneficial financial behavior in cash-flow management, credit management, savings, and investments. The study found a positive relation between financial literacy scores and "Financial Practices Index" scores. In a study of Dutch adults, van Rooij, Lusardi, and Alessie (2007) found that those with low financial literacy are more likely than others to rely on friends and family (who themselves may be ignorant) for financial advice and are less likely to invest in stocks. In a German study of mutual fund shareholders, Müller and Weber (2010) found a significant and positive relationship between financial literacy and the likelihood of using lower cost, passively managed funds. Using the 2006 Jump$tart survey, Mandell (2006) found that high school seniors who balanced their checkbooks or who never bounced a check had substantially higher financial literacy scores than other students with checking accounts.

Financial Education and Behavior

Although financial behavior seems to be positively affected by financial literacy, the effects of financial education on financial behavior are less certain. Bernheim, Garrett, and Maki (2001) found that those who took a high school financial management course in states that mandated such a course tended in middle age to save a higher proportion of their incomes than others. Cole and Shastry (2009) disputed these findings, and instead found that:

> Individuals born in states in which mandates were imposed are substantially more likely to report investment income, relative to those born in states in which mandates were not imposed. However, this holds for those who graduate from high school before the mandates went into effect. Thus, there is no increase in investment income for cohorts that were born after the mandate. (p. 19)

Using a matched sample of students who did and did not take a well-regarded high school personal finance elective offered in a Midwestern school district, Mandell and Klein (2009) found little difference in self-beneficial behavior from one to five years after graduation. Shorter interventions may actually work better. Danes (2004) reported positive changes in financial behavior immediately after and again three months after high school student exposure to the part-semester personal finance curriculum supplied to teachers by the National Endowment for Financial Education (NEFE). Self-reported changes in behavior were reported as well by Borden, Lee, Serido, and Collins (2008) in their study of a shorter intervention (Credit Wise Cats).

In contrast to these results, an analysis of high school seniors who bounced a check, a question included in the 2006 Jump$tart survey, finds that although financial literacy scores, race, and aspiration are significant determinants of such non-self-beneficial behavior, financial management education had no effect (Mandell 2006). Recent research by Norvilitis and MacLean (2010) questioned whether purely educational programming aiming to increase financial knowledge would help most students avoid debt.

The lack of success of high school classes in personal finance should come as little surprise in light of other high school programs designed to change or modify behavior in other important areas. As an example, a meta analysis by DiCenso, Guyatt, Willan, and Griffith (2002) found that educational interventions designed to reduce unwanted pregnancies among adolescents neither delayed initiation of sexual intercourse nor reduced pregnancy rates.

A number of comprehensive overviews have been written, suggesting a way to make personal finance education more effective in high school (McCormick 2009; O'Connell 2009; Atkinson 2008; and Mundy 2009). Norvilitis and MacLean (2010) suggested more individually based hands-on mentoring to help young adults avoid debt. In spite of its demonstrated ineffectiveness, Suiter and Meszaros (2005) argued against postponing financial education because non-school sources of such information may lack accuracy, and many students drop out of school before their senior year. Meier and Sprenger (2007) and Mandell and Klein (2009) found that it is important to motivate students concerning the relevance of such education for their own future living standards.

Consistent Learning

It is interesting to compare high school educational interventions by the consistency of their outcomes in teaching different concepts related to personal finance. **Table 1** looks at five types of interventions ranging from a full-semester high school class in personal finance to a full-semester course in economics to part-semester interventions in both subjects and the playing of a stock market game. Data came from the five national Jump$tart surveys of high school seniors from 2000 to 2008, which asked students about their education related to personal finance.

The worst outcomes were associated with taking a full-semester course in personal finance, where they answered only one question better than average on a consistent basis and six questions consistently below average. The single question in which these students did consistently better than average was factual, but trivial, and became less relevant over the time period studied. It was

Table 1. Number of Questions Answered Consistently Above or Below Average by Educational Intervention

Educational Intervention	Consistently Above Average	Consistently Below Average
Semester money management	1	6
Part-semester money management	2	2
Semester economics	2	1
Part-semester economics	4	1
Played stock market game	16	0

Source: Jump$tart Surveys 2000–2008.

the size of the maximum charge ($50) allowed under federal law for credit card holders whose card was lost or stolen and abused if the card issuer was notified promptly. Because most issuers voluntarily did away with this penalty, this knowledge became largely irrelevant, but the fact that it was the only question in which those who took a full-semester class did better than those who did not is probably indicative of the didactic, fact-based mode of teaching. These students did consistently worse than students who had not taken such a course in questions relating to the value of continuing one's education, calculating the months of saving needed to reach a savings objective, the importance of keeping savings needed for an imminent payment in liquid form, the ways of protecting asset value from sudden inflation, the difficulties of using bank CDs (certificates of deposit) to make payments, and the fact that those who make the smallest allowable credit card payments each month pay more in credit card charges than those who make larger payments. In short, the courses seem to have emphasized facts over reasoning.

By far, the best outcomes were associated with playing a stock market game, where students answered 16 of the 31 questions more accurately every time than did those who did not play this game. Surprisingly, these questions covered almost every area.

Students who had only a small amount of exposure to personal financial planning in high school as well as those who had at least some exposure to economics also did better than those students who took a full-semester course in personal finance.

Adults

A number of studies of adult behavior modification education have also found mixed outcomes (see Braunstein and Welch 2002; Martin 2007; O'Connell 2009; and Yoong 2010 for a general review of findings). These include the usefulness of retirement seminars. Bayer, Bernheim, and Scholz (1996) found that employer retirement seminars increased participation in and contributions to voluntary savings plans, and Lusardi and Mitchell (2006) found that retirement seminars have a positive wealth effect, but primarily for those with less wealth or education. Duflo and Saez (2003) found that retirement seminars have a positive effect on participation in retirement plans, but found the increase in contributions to be negligible. Choi, Laibson, Madrian, and Metrick (2006) and Madrian and Shea (2001) found that participants in retirement seminars had much better intentions than follow-through capabilities.

Outside of retirement planning, Elliehausen, Lundquist, and Staten (2007) found that credit counseling tended to improve both borrowing behavior and creditworthiness. Similarly, Hirad and Zorn (2001) found that pre-purchase counseling programs for prospective homebuyers decreased delinquency rates. Both of these studies reiterate the fact that financial education is most useful if it is specific to important, imminent decisions because pre-purchase motivation to learn is very high.

Recent work by Cole, Sampson, and Zia (2009) using original household survey data from India and Indonesia showed that financial literacy is a powerful predictor of demand for financial services. Cole et al. (2009) also conducted a field experiment in which unbanked households were randomly selected and exposed to a two-day financial education program focusing on bank accounts. They found that, except among uneducated and financially illiterate consumers, financial literacy training had no effect on the likelihood of opening a savings account. On the other hand, small subsidy payments to the participants had a considerable and positive effect on the likelihood of opening a bank account, regardless of the participant's financial literacy, thus demonstrating the superiority of incentives over education. According to Schreiner and Sherraden (2007), each hour of savings-related financial education given to lower income Americans resulted in additional savings of just $1.16 per participant. The effect was pretty nearly linear up to 10 hours of education, showing that more financial education results in better financial outcomes. However, since the cost of the education was $3.00 per participant hour, the authors question the efficacy of such education.

Once out of school, it is hard to provide effective education to adults who have to make imminent complex financial decisions. Although it is theoretically possible to reach adults in the workplace, Mandell (2008b) found that few employers are motivated to provide effective and disinterested financial education because it is expensive and largely unappreciated by employees as a work-related benefit.

What Type of Education Could Prevent Major Consumer Mistakes?

Because financial innovation appears to be unconstrained in spite of recent financial difficulties, we must ask about the type of financial education that is likely to be most helpful. First, we must address the question of when such education is likely to be most effective. To help frame the question, let's consider a single important example—educating consumers about the choice between a fixed- and variable-rate mortgage.

In order to educate people while we still have some control over what they study, this education would have to occur while they were still in high school, preferably right before they graduated. Because few 18-year-olds will be making home mortgage decisions for at least 10 years, and because the rapid pace of financial innovation tends to make obsolete many products in this category, we must question both the motivation of students to learn and retain these materials and the likely usefulness of such knowledge at the time of application.

Even aside from the issues of motivation and shelf life, the decision between fixed- and floating-rate mortgages is very complex, presupposing a solid working knowledge of yield curves, LIBOR rates, monetary policy, underwriting standards, and even option theory. An assumption of market efficiency may prevent needless speculation, but the optimal choice depends upon many complex and unique features of each borrower's life, including trajectory, stability and diversification of future income, asset size and composition, and future liabilities for dependents. A few courses in consumer economics are unlikely to equip a teacher to be able to handle this subject, nor will a textbook, which is often outdated well before it is printed. What exactly can you teach high school students about this subject that will equip them to make a reasonable decision when the time comes?

This example can be broadened to most other areas where consumers have made their costly mistakes, including the choice and use of unsecured and secured short- and intermediate-term credit, a home purchase, the purchase of insurance (health, life, and disability), and the choice and allocation of investment assets. It is difficult to state exactly what should be taught to primary or secondary school (or even college) students that would be helpful to them and who would be capable of teaching it.

Once we leave the area of mandatory (K–12) education, we enter voluntary education, in college or for adults in the workplace. Here, we have serious election bias in that those who are probably most in need of such education (i.e., those with less formal education, lower incomes, and less financial experience) are also least likely to want to extend their educations in this manner (Mandell

2008a). Most likely to show up at employer seminars on investing, retiring, or even consumer credit are the "fine tuners" who (1) enjoy classes and (2) tend to keep up and enjoy dealing with financial issues.

Changing Behavior

Perhaps it isn't knowledge that we wish to change as much as it is impulse control. We would like (future) consumers to save more, borrow less, and carefully research important financial decisions—in short, we want them to defer immediate gratification. In the famous "marshmallow" study by Walter Mischel and his colleagues (Mischel, Shoda, and Rodriguez 1989), we learn that small children who are capable of deferring immediate gratification (i.e., resisting the immediate consumption of a pre-lunch marshmallow in exchange for two) become far more successful as students than those who yield to immediate temptation. Later, follow-up studies (Mischel and Ayduk 2004) found that they also became much more successful adults. Those who defer tend to save more for the future, invest more in their own human capital as well as in financial capital, and borrow less for non-capital items. They tend to employ, in Laibson's terms, a lower discount rate for future returns, both positive and negative (Laibson 1997).

If we assume that both "desirable" and undesirable behaviors can be learned, we must ask how and at what age. Many desirable behaviors are instilled by parents through operant conditioning before children are capable of relevant cognition. Children are toilet "trained," not educated, and are trained to brush their teeth well before they understand why. It is likely that attitudes toward thrift (i.e., gratification deferral) are also partially formed during these early years as part of a family's culture that might include a prohibition against taking a second helping before all family members have had a first. If the most important determinants of future financial "success" are those relating to impulse control, it would suggest that our focus should turn from the "financial literacy" education of high school students to behavior modification of children in kindergarten and early grades. This is supported by the work of child development experts who focus on the early development of financial behavior:

> There is no such thing as a purely financial behavior. Actions such as saving or spending have important emotional components. There are also strong social norms governing financial behaviors. Moreover, financial behaviors may be simply habitual; routines or practices that people have adopted without explicit justification. The basic socio-cultural perspective on development is that young children will initially participate in practices without really understanding their bases. (Holden, Kalish, Scheinholtz, Dietrich, and Novak 2009, p. 32)

School-based savings accounts helped develop early savings behavior decades ago but have been almost eliminated by a variety of factors, including privacy laws, laws in many states prohibiting children from controlling their own bank accounts, mistrust of school employees, and bank functional cost analysis, which showed (at one time) school-based accounts to be unprofitable.

Many parents give their children a regular allowance, thinking that it will teach them self-control and the need to budget. Unfortunately, it does not make them more financially literate (Marshall and Magruder 1960). Studies of allowances show that children who had to work for their money, either by doing chores for their allowance or even "badgering" parents for it, tended to end up more financially literate (Mandell 2004) and more willing to work for a living (Mortimer, Dennehy, Lee, and Finch 1994) than their counterparts who received weekly "entitlements."

Some Positive Results from Financial Education

Research over the past 15 years has yielded some positive outcomes from school-based financial education. Student scores on the Jump$tart national exam were boosted by about 2% as a result of having trained teachers teaching required semester-long courses in personal finance (Mandell 2006). Students who have played a stock market game in class tended to score about 3 percentage points higher than others (Mandell 2009a). There may also be a greatly lagged but positive effect of classes in personal finance on behavior reported by Bernheim, Garrett, and Maki (2001), Mandell (2009b), and others, sometimes occurring decades after completion of the education.

In addition, some documented success has been shown in recent experiments in education involving charter schools, where discipline and gratification deferral are enforced through strict rules of behavior, including the wearing of uniforms (Hoxby, Murarka, and Kang 2009). However, our willingness and ability as a society to scale these experiments up to the entire population must be questioned.

Other Methods to Prevent Costly Consumer Financial Mistakes

It is too early to give up totally on school-based financial education, although the difficulties inherent in successful implementation direct us to alternative solutions to avoid major consumer financial mistakes. A number of solutions have been proposed:

- Well-designed default products could help most consumers achieve their primary financial goals without having to make complex financial decisions. Some default products use well-tested principles of behavioral economics, such as opt-out rather than opt-in retirement plans. Others, such as target-date 401(k) asset allocation plans or Aspen Institute's proposed RS+ (Real Savings +) plans (Mandell, Perun, Mensah, and O'Mara 2009), make continuing and ongoing financial decisions for consumers automatically and (presumably) in their best interests.

- Simple "plain vanilla" products could be created, vetted, and blessed for each major financial product category for consumers who are not capable of making more complex financial choices. These might include, for example, a "standard" home mortgage, which would be fixed-rate for 30 years without prepayment penalty.

- A government agency could scrutinize financial products before they are offered, ensuring that they are presented in an honest, comprehensible manner, and place income, net worth, or even knowledge constraints on those to whom the more complex products may be offered.

- There is also a "middle way," which could combine the most effective aspects of financial education with a set of default, plain, or protected products, pending, of course, the legislative outcome of proposed restrictions on unfettered consumer choice.

Conclusions and Implications

During a period of diminishing economic resources, it is especially important to carefully evaluate the costs and benefits of any proposed, new social initiative. Proposals to mandate the teaching of personal finance come at a time when real expenditures on public education are either stagnant or falling, teachers are being laid off in many states, and the resources needed to provide even basic education appear to be inadequate. Consequently, the diversion of educational resources into a new area must be justified by a high likely payoff.

Unfortunately, there is little evidence that school-based financial education has had any durable effect on increasing knowledge and self-beneficial decision making. Nor is there much evidence that it is effective in changing behavior in a positive manner. These findings are particularly true at the secondary school and college levels. At the primary level, there is some evidence that knowledge, attitudes, and even behavior appear to be most susceptible to intervention at an earlier age. Behavioral patterns appear to be most efficiently influenced by pre-cognitive training, which suggests pre-school interventions.

From a policy perspective, these findings would suggest that the mandated teaching of personal finance at the secondary level be strongly reconsidered, particularly as schools are forced to lay off teachers and restructure programs.

These programs should not be resumed until there is solid evidence that effective techniques are known and there are enough properly trained teachers to deliver effective personal financial education.

Here, we speak not just about the waste of educational resources. A tremendous amount of corporate funding is being spent on questionable and redundant financial education curricula, generally by the 501(c)(3) foundation arms of large financial institutions. We must ask if CRA (Community Reinvestment Act) credit should be given to banks whose foundations provide funding for financial education unless they can demonstrate that such education is more valuable to low- and moderate-income consumers than providing affordable access to the banking system.

BIBLIOGRAPHY

Atkinson, Adele. 2008. "Evidence of Impact: An Overview of Financial Education Evaluations." *Consumer Research*, no. 68 (July).

Bayer, Patrick J., B. Douglas Bernheim, and John Karl Scholz. 1996. "The Effects of Financial Education in the Workplace: Evidence from a Survey of Employers." NBER Working Paper 5655 (July).

Bernheim, B. Douglas, Daniel M. Garrett, and Dean M. Maki. 2001. "Education and Saving: The Long-Term Effects of High School Financial Curriculum Mandates." *Journal of Public Economics*, vol. 80, no. 3 (June):435–465.

Borden, Lynne M., Sun-A Lee, Joyce Serido, and Dawn Collins. 2008. "Changing College Students' Financial Knowledge, Attitudes, and Behavior through Seminar Participation." *Journal of Family and Economic Issues*, vol. 29, no. 1 (March):23–40.

Braunstein, Sandra, and Carolyn Welch. 2002. "Financial Literacy: An Overview of Practice, Research, and Policy." *Federal Reserve Bulletin* (November):445–457.

Campbell, John Y. 2006. "Household Finance." *Journal of Finance*, vol. 61, no. 4 (August):1553–1604.

Chen, Haiyang, and Ronald P. Volpe. 1998. "An Analysis of Personal Financial Literacy among College Students." *Financial Services Review*, vol. 7, no. 2:107–128.

Choi, James, David Laibson, Brigitte Madrian, and Andrew Metrick. 2006. "Saving for Retirement on the Path of Least Resistance." In *Behavioral Public Finance: Toward a New Agenda.* Edited by Edward J. McCaffrey and Joel Slemrod. New York: Russell Sage Foundation.

Christelis, Dimitris, Tullio Jappelli, and Mario Padula. 2010. "Cognitive Abilities and Portfolio Choice." *European Economic Review*, vol. 54, no. 1 (January):18–38.

Cole, Shawn, and Kartini Shastry. 2009. "Smart Money: The Effect of Education, Cognitive Ability and Financial Literacy on Financial Market Participation." Working Paper 09-071, Harvard Business School (14 January).

Cole, Shawn, Thomas Sampson, and Bilal Zia. 2009. "Financial Literacy, Financial Decisions, and the Demand for Financial Services: Evidence from India and Indonesia." Working Paper 09-117, Harvard Business School (February).

Council for Economic Education. 2009. *Survey of the States: Economic, Personal Finance & Entrepreneurship Education in Our Nation's Schools in 2009, a Report Card.* New York: Council for Economic Education.

Danes, Sharon M. 2004. *Evaluation of the NEFE High School Financial Planning Program® 2003–2004.* Denver: National Endowment for Financial Education.

Danes, Sharon M., and Tahira K. Hira. 1987. "Money Management Knowledge of College Students." *Journal of Student Financial Aid*, vol. 17, no. 1:4–16.

De Mello Ferreira, Vera Rita. 2010. "Financial Education—Can Economic Psychology and Behavioral Economics Help Improve It?" Paper presented at the OECD-Bank of Italy Symposium on Financial Literacy: Improving Financial Education Efficiency, Rome (June).

de Meza, David, Bernd Irlenbusch, and Diane Reyniers. 2008. "Financial Capability: A Behavioural Economics Perspective." *Consumer Research*, no. 69 (July).

DiCenso, A., G. Guyatt, A. Willan, and L. Griffith. 2002. "Interventions to Reduce Unintended Pregnancies among Adolescents: Systematic Review of Randomized Controlled Trials." *British Medical Journal*, vol. 324, no. 7351 (15 June):1426–1430.

Duflo, Esther, and Emmanuel Saez. 2003. "The Role of Information and Social Interactions in Retirement Plan Decisions: Evidence from a Randomized Experiment." *Quarterly Journal of Economics*, vol. 118, no. 3 (August):815–842.

Elliehausen, Gregory, E. Christopher Lundquist, and Michael E. Staten. 2007. "The Impact of Credit Counseling on Subsequent Borrower Behavior." *Journal of Consumer Affairs*, vol. 41, no. 1 (Summer):1–28.

Hilgert, Marianne A., Jeanne M. Hogarth, and Sondra G. Beverly. 2003. "Household Financial Management: The Connection between Knowledge and Behavior." *Federal Reserve Bulletin*, vol. 89, no. 7:309–322.

Hira, Tahira K. 2002. "Current Financial Environment and Financial Practices: Implications for Financial Health." *Journal of Family and Consumer Sciences*, vol. 94, no. 1 (January):1–4.

Hirad, Abdighani, and Peter M. Zorn. 2001. "A Little Knowledge Is a Good Thing: Empirical Evidence of the Effectiveness of Pre-Purchasing Homeownership Counseling." McLean, VA: Freddie Mac (22 May).

Holden, Karen, Charles Kalish, Laura Scheinholtz, Deanna Dietrich, and Beatriz Novak. 2009. "Financial Literacy Programs Targeted on Pre-School Children: Development and Evaluation." Working Paper 2009-09, La Follette School, University of Wisconsin–Madison.

Hoxby, Caroline M., Sonali Murarka, and Jenny Kang. 2009. "How New York City's Charter Schools Affect Achievement." The New York City Charter Schools Evaluation Project (September): www.nber.org/~schools/charterschoolseval/how_NYC_charter_schools_affect_achievement_sept2009.pdf.

Katayama, Kentaro. 2006. "Why Does Japan's Saving Rate Decline So Rapidly?" Report for the Policy Research Institute, Ministry of Finance, Tokyo. PRI Discussion Paper Series, no. 06A-30.

Laibson, David. 1997. "Golden Eggs and Hyperbolic Discounting." *Quarterly Journal of Economics*, vol. 112, no. 2 (May):443–478.

Loibl, Cäzilia. 2008. *Survey of Financial Education in Ohio's Schools.* Columbus, OH: Research Report, The Ohio State University.

Lusardi, Annamaria, and Olivia S. Mitchell. 2006. "Financial Literacy and Planning: Implications for Retirement Wellbeing." Working paper, The Wharton School of the University of Pennsylvania, Pension Research Council Working Paper 1 (October).

Lusardi, Annamaria, Punam Anand Keller, and Adam M. Keller. 2009. "New Ways to Make People Save: A Social Marketing Approach." In *Overcoming the Saving Slump: How to Increase the Effectiveness of Financial Education and Saving Programs.* Edited by Annamaria Lusardi. Chicago: University of Chicago Press.

Lusardi, Annamaria, Olivia S. Mitchell, and Vilsa Curto. 2010. "Financial Literacy among the Young." *Journal of Consumer Affairs*, vol. 44, no. 2 (Summer):358–380.

Madrian, Brigitte, and Dennis Shea. 2001. "Preaching to the Converted and Converting Those Taught: Financial Education in the Workplace." Working paper, University of Chicago.

Mandell, Lewis. 2001. *Improving Financial Literacy: What Schools and Parents Can and Cannot Do—Results of the 2000 National Jump$tart Survey.* Washington, DC: Jump$tart Coalition.

———. 2002. *Financial Literacy: A Growing Problem—Results of the 2002 National Jump$tart Survey.* Washington, DC: Jump$tart Coalition.

———. 2004. *Financial Literacy: Are We Improving—Results of the 2004 National Jump$tart Survey.* Washington, DC: Jump$tart Coalition.

———. 2006. *Financial Literacy—Improving Education.* Washington, DC: Jump$tart Coalition.

———. 2008a. *Financial Education in the Workplace—A Cost–Benefit Analysis.* Washington, DC: New America Foundation.

———. 2008b. *The Financial Literacy of Young American Adults: Results of the 2008 National Jump$tart Coalition Survey of High School Seniors and College Students.* Washington, DC: Jump$tart Coalition.

————. 2009a. *The Financial Literacy of Young American Adults: Results of the 2008 National Jump$tart Coalition Survey of High School Seniors and College Students.* Washington, DC: Jump$tart Coalition.

————. 2009b. *The Impact of Financial Education in High School and College on Financial Literacy and Subsequent Financial Decision Making.* Nashville, TN: American Economic Association (4 January): www.aeaweb.org/assa/2009/retrieve.php?pdfid=507.

————. 2009c. *Two Cheers for School-Based Financial Education.* Washington, DC: Aspen Institute Initiative on Financial Security (17 June): www.aspeninstitute.org/publications/two-cheer-school-based-financial-education.

Mandell, Lewis, and Linda S. Klein. 2009. "The Impact of Financial Literacy Education on Subsequent Financial Behavior." *Journal of Financial Counseling and Planning*, vol. 20, no. 1:15–24.

Mandell, Lewis, Pamela Perun, Lisa Mensah, and Raymond O'Mara. 2009. *Real Savings +: An Automatic Investment Option for the Automatic IRA.* Washington, DC: Aspen Institute.

Marshall, Helen R., and Lucille Magruder. 1960. "Relations between Parents' Money Education Practices and Children's Knowledge and Use of Money." *Child Development*, vol. 31, no. 2 (June):253–284.

Martin, Matthew. 2007. "A Literature Review on the Effectiveness of Financial Education." Working Paper 07-3, Federal Reserve Bank of Richmond (15 June).

McCormick, Martha H. 2009. "The Effectiveness of Youth Financial Education: A Review of the Literature." *Journal of Financial Counseling and Planning*, vol. 20, no. 1:70–83.

Meier, Stephen, and Charles Sprenger. 2007. "Selection into Financial Literacy Programs: Evidence from a Field Study." Discussion Paper No. 07-5, Federal Reserve Bank of Boston.

Mischel, Walter, and Ozlem Ayduk. 2004. "Willpower in a Cognitive-Affective Processing System: The Dynamics of Delay of Gratification." In *Handbook of Self-Regulation: Research, Theory, and Applications.* Edited by R.F. Baumeister and K.D. Vohs. New York: Guilford.

Mischel, W., Y. Shoda, and M.L. Rodriguez. 1989. "Delay of Gratification in Children." *Science*, vol. 244, no. 4907 (May):933–938.

Mortimer, Jeylan T., Katherine Dennehy, Chaimun Lee, and Michael D. Finch. 1994. "Economic Socialization in the American Family: The Prevalence, Distribution and Consequences of Allowance Arrangements." *Family Relations*, vol. 43, no. 1 (January):23–29.

Müller, Sebastian, and Martin Weber. 2010. "Financial Literacy and Mutual Fund Investments: Who Buys Actively Managed Funds?" *Schmalenbach Business Review*, vol. 62 (April):126–153.

Mundy, Shaun. 2009. *Financial Education Programs in Schools: Analysis of Selected Current Programmes and Literature—Draft Recommendations for Best Practices.* Report, Organisation for Economic Co-Operation and Development.

NASB. 2006. *Who Owns Our Children?* Alexandria, VA: National Association of State Boards of Education.

Norvilitis, Jill M., and Michael G. MacLean. 2010. "The Role of Parents in College Students' Financial Behaviors and Attitudes." *Journal of Economic Psychology*, vol. 31, no. 1 (February):55–63.

Norvilitis, Jill M., Bernard Szablicki, and Sandy B. Wilson. 2003. "Factors Influencing Levels of Credit Card Debt in College Students." *Journal of Applied Social Psychology*, vol. 33, no. 5 (May):935–947.

Norvilitis, Jill M., M.M. Merwin, T.M. Osberg, P.V. Roehling, P. Young, and M.M. Kamas. 2006. "Personality Factors, Money Attitudes, Financial Knowledge and Credit Card Debt in College Students." *Journal of Applied Social Psychology*, vol. 36, no. 6 (June):1395–1413.

O'Connell, Alison. 2009. *Evaluating the Effectiveness of Financial Education Programmes.* Report, Organisation for Economic Co-Operation and Development.

OECD. 2005. *Improving Financial Literacy: Analysis of Issues and Policies.* Report, Organisation for Economic Co-Operation and Development.

Public Interest Research Group Education Fund (PIRG). 2008. "The Campus Credit Card Trap" (March).

Roberts, James A., and E. Eli Jones. 2001. "Money Attitudes, Credit Card Use, and Compulsive Buying among American College Students." *Journal of Consumer Affairs*, vol. 35, no. 21 (Winter):213–240.

Sallie Mae. 2009. "How Undergraduate Students Use Credit Cards." Sallie Mae's National Study of Usage Rates and Trends (April).

Schreiner, Mark, and Michael Sherraden. 2007. *Can the Poor Save? Saving and Asset Building in Individual Development Accounts.* New Brunswick, NJ: Transaction Publishers.

Seaward, Hamish G.W., and Simon Kemp. 2000. "Optimism Bias and Student Debt." *New Zealand Journal of Psychology*, vol. 29, no. 1 (June):17–19.

Staten, Michael. 2002. *The Impact of Credit Counseling on Subsequent Borrower Credit Usage and Payment Behavior.* Washington, DC: Georgetown University Credit Research Monograph, no. 36.

Suiter, Mary, and Bonnie T. Meszaros. 2005. "Teaching about Savings and Investing in the Elementary and Middle School Grades." *Social Education*, vol. 69, no. 2 (March):92–95.

U.S. Department of the Treasury. 2008. "Annual Report to the President." President's Advisory Council on Financial Literacy.

van Rooij, Maarten, Annamaria Lusardi, and Rob Alessie. 2007. "Financial Literacy and Stock Market Participation." Paper presented at the Italian Congress of Econometrics and Empirical Economics, Rimini (25–26 January).

Varcoe, Karen, Shirley Peterson, Charles Go, and Margaret Johns. 2002. "Teen Financial Literacy Evaluated to Develop Outreach Materials." *California Agriculture*, vol. 56, no. 2 (March–April):65–68.

Volpe, Ronald P., Haiyang Chen, and Sheen Liu. 2006. "An Analysis of the Importance of Personal Finance Topics and the Level of Knowledge Possessed by Working Adults." *Financial Services Review*, vol. 15, no. 1 (Spring):81–99.

Willis, Lauren E. 2008. "Against Financial-Literacy Education." *Iowa Law Review*, vol. 94:197–285.

Yoong, Joanne. 2010. "Making Financial Education More Effective: Lessons from Behavioral Economics." Paper presented at the OECD-Bank of Italy Symposium on Financial Literacy: Improving Financial Education Efficiency, Rome (June).

Session 5: Financial Education: What Have We Learned So Far?

Financial Education: Lessons Not Learned and Lessons Learned

Lauren Willis
Professor
Loyola Law School Los Angeles

Lessons Not Learned

A plethora of financial education programs have been tried in a host of settings. Courses are offered or even required by elementary schools and high schools, the military and other government agencies, employers, community and faith-based organizations, the courts, and firms selling financial products. The underlying theory is that imparting information about financial concepts, products, and transactions and training consumers to use that information will produce a populace with the knowledge and skills necessary to function well in the financial marketplace. Most educators, along with an emerging cadre of financial mental health professionals (Maton, Maton, and Martin 2010), recognize that this alone will not produce desired behavior. They add to the programs a sort of financial therapy to motivate and give confidence to consumers to use their newfound knowledge and skills. The theoretical result is good financial behavior, meaning the decisions and actions our society requires for households to enjoy financial well-being. The causal chain envisioned (**Exhibit 1**) goes from financial education/therapy, to financial literacy and mental health, to good financial behavior, to household financial well-being.

Does financial education work as hoped? Empirical evidence does not support the theory. Some (but not all) studies show a positive correlation between financial education and financial knowledge or between financial knowledge and financial outcomes. But no strong empirical evidence validates the theory that financial education leads to household well-being through the pathway of increasing literacy leading to improved behavior (Hathaway and Khatiwada 2008; Willis 2009; Gale and Levine 2011).

Exhibit 1.   The Intended Pathway

Financial Education	+	Financial Therapy
	↓	
Financial Literacy	+	Financial Mental Health
Knowledge and Skills	+	Motivation and Confidence
	↓	
Good Financial Behavior: decisions and actions society requires		
	↓	
Household Financial Well-Being		

To the contrary, a number of studies indicate that financial education may have either no positive effect on behavior and outcomes or even a small negative effect. Holding potentially confounding factors constant, the only statistically significant effect of mandatory personal financial training on soldiers was that they adopted worse household budgeting behaviors after the training than before it (Bell, Gorin, and Hogarth 2009, p. 20 and Table 16). When financial education was mandated for bankruptcy debtors, they were less likely to meet their bankruptcy plans; this leaves them substantially worse off financially because rather than paying only the court's assessment of what they could afford on their debts and then having the remaining debt discharged to give them a fresh start, debtors who do not meet their plans lose the protection of the court and are saddled with the entire original debt owed (Braucher 2001). Youth who play a stock market game as part of a high school personal finance course increase their financial knowledge, but they are less thrifty than their peers (Mandell 2008). Several studies show financial fraud victims to be more financially knowledgeable than nonvictims (Moore 2003; National Association of Securities Dealers 2006). When borrowers who have been counseled that the mortgage terms they have been offered are poor attempt to renegotiate with their lenders, on average, they end up with terms that are no better (Agarwal, Amromin, Ben-David, Chomsisengphet, and Evanoff 2009). Youth who took a personal finance course in high school do not report better financial behavior several years later than youth who did not take the course (Mandell and Klein 2009). Adults who attended public schools where they were required to take personal financial courses were found to have no better financial outcomes than adults who were not required to take such courses (Cole and Shastry 2008).

Insurmountable Barriers to Effective Financial Education

Changing behavior is extremely difficult to do, and financial education is not the only example of an expensive failed attempt. For example, driver's education for high school students does not reduce these students' traffic accidents; in fact, by encouraging teen drivers at younger ages, it actually increases accidents (Vernick, Li, Ogaitis, MacKenzie, Baker, and Gielen 1999). Are there particular reasons why financial education programs fail to change behavior in the manner intended? Why do some programs appear to lead to worse outcomes? Is it merely that we have not developed the right delivery method? Although some programs appear weak on the surface, there are many reasons why even the best designed and most zealously implemented financial education programs are destined for failure.

The first hurdle is the speed and dynamism of the financial marketplace. Yesterday, the new product was the option adjustable-rate mortgage (ARM); today, it is the medical credit card. It was once common wisdom that people should have a rainy day fund equal to three months of expenses, but given typical unemployment durations experienced today, that is not enough. Consumers who attend a course in high school will not face most of their lifetime decisions about credit, insurance, and investment until many years have passed. At that point, the financial marketplace will most likely have changed so much that the information they learned in high school may be outdated and misleading. Major personal finance decisions are episodic; consumers do not keep up with changes in the ordinary course of walking down the grocery aisle.

Although the "solution" to this might appear to be frequent education to keep consumer knowledge current, many people do not want to spend their time or effort on financial instruction. In surveys, they often say they want more education, but when it is offered, take-up is low. When credit card issuers warned thousands of cardholders that they were at risk of delinquency and offered them a free online financial literacy course, only 28 (0.4%) attempted to log onto the website and only 2 (0.03%) completed the course (Brown and Gartner 2007).

Consumers so strongly prefer not to participate that a major effect of an Illinois law that required a one-hour session of free financial counseling before obtaining particular types of mortgages was that consumers switched to other mortgage products to avoid the session (Agarwal et al. 2009). Ironically, those who participate voluntarily in financial counseling already have more financial knowledge, better budgeting and planning skills, and personalities more conducive to good money management (lower financial discount rates) than those who do not participate (Meier and Sprenger 2007; Garman, Kim, Kratzer, Brunson, and Joo 1999). Nonparticipation could be rational; the value of these programs to those who choose not to attend could well be less than, for example, income-producing activities they would otherwise choose to do with their time.

Another reason financial education is unlikely to produce household financial well-being is that consumers' knowledge, comprehension, skills, and willpower are far too low in comparison with what our society demands. Independent decisions about credit, insurance, and investments demand not only financial knowledge and skills but also numeracy, linguistic literacy, and the ability to make informed predictions about the future. A readability assessment of credit card holder agreements found that information regarding grace periods, balance computation methods, and payment allocation methods was written at a 15th-grade or higher level. Almost half of U.S. adults cannot read beyond the eighth-grade level (U.S. GAO 2006). That is simply too large a gap for financial literacy education to bridge. Moreover, financial education cannot teach people to predict their own future income, expenses, and health or future market performance—such as interest rates, investment returns, and inflation—with any reasonable degree of certainty. Even experts disagree about what the future will hold (e.g., Shiller 2006).

Furthermore, making financial decisions typically requires both substantial reasoning and self-control. But deliberation and self-control are performed by the same area of the brain, which has limited resources (Baumeister, Sparks, Stillman, and Vohs 2008). Impulsiveness has a substantial biological component and may negatively affect financial decisions; particular variants of one gene, for example, are associated with higher credit card debt (De Neve and Fowler 2009). More broadly, genetics appears to influence a number of financial behaviors (Cesarini, Johannesson, Lichtenstein, Sandewall, and Wallace 2010). These genetic influences are likely to be difficult to overcome with financial education.

Although "rules of thumb" are easy to teach, financial product offerings today are too complex and consumer circumstances too diverse for simple rules. For example, when taught to diversify, many consumers respond by taking the menu of investments being offered to them and dividing their savings evenly amongst the options (Benartzi and Thaler 2001). Understanding how to balance asset classes within a portfolio requires knowing far more than a rule of thumb. Such rules as "never spend retirement savings" or "never miss a mortgage payment" are poor lessons in some circumstances. When defaulting on an underwater mortgage costs a consumer less from a reduced credit score than the amount by which the mortgage is underwater, for example, these rules should be violated on financial grounds alone.

Other intractable impediments to the efficacy of financial education are the triggers for nonrational behavior that pervade financial decision making. Even consumers with abundant financial knowledge and skills make mistakes surprisingly often (Choi, Laibson, and Madrian 2010; van de Venter and Michayluk 2008). Although these triggers for poor financial decisions do not affect all consumers to the same degree, that itself is a barrier to making financial education effective. For example, some consumers are plagued by overconfidence in their own abilities and others by underconfidence. In one study, over 29% of respondents who assessed their own financial literacy as being at the highest level objectively tested in the bottom quartile and over 5% who self-assessed their literacy at the lowest level tested in the top quartile (Lusardi and Mitchell 2009, Table 4B). Financial education/therapy designed to boost or reduce confidence could help some consumers and hinder others.

One common trigger is information and choice overload: Consumers are faced with a tremendous number of choices in the financial marketplace and reams of information about each one, which can lead to oversimplified decision strategies or inertia (a failure to make any decision) (Sethi-Iyengar, Huberman, and Jiang 2004). Personal finance decisions often involve high stakes and require recognizing susceptibility to unemployment, illness, and other financially taxing events. Many people respond with overconfidence about their own probability of experiencing misfortunes (Weinstein 1999), leading to decisions that fail to realistically account for these (Stephens 2004). Most people find financial decisions—and even financial education—stressful (Caplin and Leahy 2003), and stress occupies cognitive resources, reducing decision quality (Keinan 1987).

Financial decisions are always, at least in part, about the future, and they must be made in the face of uncertainty. But the further into the future or the more uncertain the outcome, the less decision weight people place on events (Trope, Liberman, and Wakslak 2007), leading to a failure to plan for uncertain future events even when these events could have serious financial consequences. Present-biased time preferences are correlated with poorer financial outcomes (Hastings and Mitchell 2011). Finally, many important financial transactions are conducted in face-to-face settings with a salesperson, and social mores trigger trust in and deference to the apparent expert sitting across the table (Cialdini 2001). Salespeople often have incentives to sell financial products that are not in consumers' best interests.

Giving consumers more information through financial education may produce only the "illusion of knowledge." When people are given more information about investments, for example, they become overconfident in their ability to invest well, believing that the information gives them more knowledge even when it does not (Barber and Odean 2001). Overconfidence about one's financial acumen appears significantly more prevalent than underconfidence among Americans (Lusardi and Mitchell 2009, Table 4B). Many of the studies showing paradoxical effects of financial education—the finding that soldiers given financial training engage in worse budgeting behaviors, for example—are likely the result of the programs' role in exacerbating participants' overconfidence. In one study, consumers who attended retirement-related financial classes thought their literacy had increased, but their scores on financial tests did not (Hershey, Walsh, Brougham, Carter, and Farrell 1998). The aphorism that a little knowledge is a dangerous thing may also be driving the results that show victims of financial fraud to be more financially knowledgeable than nonvictims.

The financial industry has the means and motivation to run circles around financial educators. Consumers are most open to learning at the time they need to use the information. These "teachable moments" are also moments when consumers are under the influence of the sellers of financial products. Even when financial education has been given very close in time to the transaction, consumers often cannot outwit salespeople. When they could not avoid the counseling session required by the Illinois law noted earlier, those consumers who were advised that the mortgage terms they had been offered were poor often renegotiated with their lenders and received different terms, but the new terms were no better than their original offers, on average (Agarwal et al. 2009).

A final barrier to effective financial education is that a substantial portion of the population has unpredictable and generally insufficient income and assets on which they might use any literacy they might gain. Over 40% of Americans report that they often do not have enough money to make ends meet (Pew Research Center for the People & the Press 2009). With nothing to save or invest, knowing how compound interest works or the difference between a stock and a bond is unhelpful. About 9% of the population is currently involuntarily unemployed, and a like number are working fewer hours than they seek (Gallup 2011). Even prior to the financial crisis, employees in many sectors faced unpredictable working hours; nearly all part-time employees and 14% of full-time employees have hours that fluctuate from week to week or month to month (Lambert and Henly 2009). With an unpredictable income stream, financial planning is largely impossible. The idea that financial education will lift all boats misses the point that many Americans do not have a boat.

Alternative Pathways from Financial Education Programs to Household Well-Being

Although financial education has not been proven to directly improve household well-being in the manner theorized, some programs may have had positive effects through different mechanisms.

Math Instruction. Numeracy is highly correlated with retirement savings (Banks, O'Dea, and Oldfield 2010), mortgage performance (Gerardi, Goette, and Meier 2010), and wealth (Smith, McArdle, and Willis 2010). For example, one study of loan defaults found that low levels of numeracy were strongly related to mortgage default, *ceteris paribus*, whereas knowledge of financial concepts had no relationship to default (Gerardi et al. 2010). Those financial education programs that teach math skills in addition to financial concepts may have positive effects.

Financial Counseling. Although "counseling" can include attempts to educate participants, counselors often take actions on behalf of their clients. That is, the role of the counselor is often more akin to a hands-on financial adviser than an educator. As some homeownership counselors have admitted, counselor interventions on behalf of consumers are probably more effective than their interactions with consumers (Mallach 2000).

One study cited as evidence of the effectiveness of financial education actually involved only two classes but two years of monthly one-on-one counseling sessions, followed by swift intervention by the counselor whenever the borrower fell 15 days behind on a payment (Agarwal, Amromin, Ben-David, Chomsisengphet, and Evanoff 2010). The counselors also performed screening and channeling functions, permitting only those participants in the program whom the counselors deemed capable of obtaining mortgages and offering them only fixed-rate products. That is, the participants did not decide for themselves whether they could handle a mortgage or which product would be best suited to their needs, but rather, the counselor decided for them. Regardless of whether participants learned anything from the two classes, the screening, channeling, and swift intervention by the counselor upon default may have led to reduced foreclosure rates for these consumers.

Commitment Devices and Automaticity. Many financial education programs also give participants access to a variety of commitment devices or devices through which financial steps will be taken for the consumer automatically. Commitment devices and automaticity both are ways of overcoming present-biased time preferences, bounded willpower, and inertia. Although many participants in financial education programs express an intention to change behavior, few follow through on their own (Choi, Laibson, Madrian, and Metrick 2006). However, when employees are automatically enrolled in retirement savings plans, enrollment can increase by 50% or more (Choi, Laibson, Madrian, and Metrick 2001). When employees can pre-commit to placing a portion of future raises into retirement savings, savings increase substantially (Thaler and Benartzi 2004). When bankruptcy courts require debtors' payments under their bankruptcy plans to be directly deducted from their paychecks, this increases plan completion rates, whereas financial education does not (Braucher 2001).

Product Deterrence. Some programs appear to increase household financial well-being not because they teach consumers about finance but because they lead consumers to stay away from particular products to avoid the counseling and/or they lead lenders to withdraw the products to avoid having their sales practices examined by a counselor. The Illinois law noted earlier had both effects (Agarwal et al. 2009).

Increased Assets or Decreased Expenses. A variety of programs provide direct monetary assistance to consumers alongside education through increasing participant assets or decreasing participant expenses. For example, some financial education programs that aim to encourage savings use matching funds to convince consumers to save more, whether in a bank account or a retirement account (Abt Associates 2004). Homebuyer education programs often reduce the expense of a mortgage through down payment assistance or reduced mortgage interest rates (Quercia and Wachter 1996). Rather than the education leading to literacy leading to improved household welfare, it may have been the monetary assistance that generated any positive program results.

Alternatives to Financial Education Programs

A number of alternative public policies to improve household financial health are suggested by these indirect, unintended pathways from financial education programs to financial well-being (**Exhibit 2**).

At the input stage, rather than attempting to increase financial literacy, we might focus on increasing the numeracy levels of consumers through *math education and prenatal interventions*. Although increasing numeracy might be achieved by the math instruction component of financial education programs, better math programs in the public schools could be more efficacious. Math ability is lower for those with very low birth weight (Taylor, Espy, and Anderson 2009) or in-utero alcohol exposure (Rasmussen and Bisanz 2009). Programs targeted at improving fetal brain development might be more effective in increasing numeracy and improving financial behavior than financial education.

At the next stage of the model, rather than hoping that consumers will acquire knowledge, skills, confidence, and motivation to manage their own financial affairs, we might arm consumers with independent, hands-on financial advisers. This would require the development of a well-regulated professional class of unbiased advisers available to consumers at all income levels.

Exhibit 2.   Alternative Pathways to Financial Well-Being

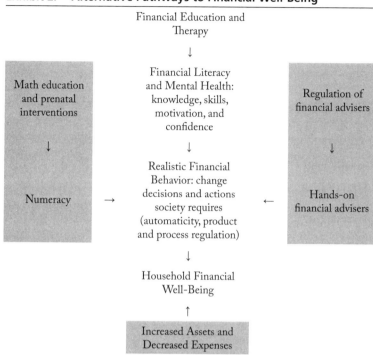

We might then replace current financial education programs with programs to teach consumers when they need expert help, how to locate competent and trustworthy advisers, and how to implement adviser instructions.

The design of a financial adviser program must be done carefully. The counseling sessions required by the Illinois law noted earlier did not help consumers because consumers could not effectively use the counselors' advice in their renegotiations with lenders (Agarwal et al. 2009). The program in which counselors determined whether and which mortgage product their clients could obtain was successful (Agarwal et al. 2010). Similarly, giving low-income families personalized college financial aid eligibility information had no effect on financial aid application rates. But actively helping the families complete the forms increased both the application rate and the rate of college enrollment (Bettinger, Long, Oreopoulos, and Sanbonmatsu 2009). Thus, to be effective, passively giving consumers personalized information or advice may not be enough. Instead, advisers would need to have a hands-on relationship with their clients' finances in which the advisers could take actions to implement financial plans for their clients.

Giving consumers access to commitment devices and automaticity or deterring firms from offering or consumers from accepting poor financial products all go to the financial behavior stage of the model. Each of these has the effect of making the financial decisions and actions that society requires of consumers less demanding, thereby transforming the meaning of good financial behavior into *realistic financial behavior* that consumers are capable of achieving. If we were to focus directly on changing this stage of the model, we might regulate what products can be sold and to whom they can be sold, rather than depending on education to enable consumers to select appropriate financial products for themselves. Regulating the financial product sales process by prohibiting compensation schemes that reward salespeople for selling consumers products that are not in the consumers' best interests would have a similar effect, and such regulation would place the onus of determining which products are appropriate for whom on firms, which could be in a better position to make this determination than the government. We might also provide automaticity and commitment devices to consumers, rather than hoping that education will motivate consumers to remember to make payments or to put aside savings every month. Social Security and unemployment insurance are examples of automatic devices that commit all income-earning Americans to "saving" a portion of their paychecks for retirement and unemployment spells.

Finally, the financial well-being of households might be directly enhanced through *increased assets or decreased expenses.* Money currently spent on ineffective financial education programs might do more for households, particularly low-income households, if used to bolster their balance sheets. For those households without a boat, the first step might be to give them one.

BIBLIOGRAPHY

Abt Associates. 2004. "Evaluation of the American Dream Demonstration, Final Evaluation Report." Prepared for the Ford Foundation (August).

Agarwal, Sumit, Gene Amromin, Itzhak Ben-David, Souphala Chomsisengphet, and Douglas D. Evanoff. 2009. "Do Financial Counseling Mandates Improve Mortgage Choice and Performance? Evidence from a Legislative Experiment." Working Paper 2009-07, Federal Reserve Bank of Chicago (October).

———. 2010. "Learning to Cope: Voluntary Financial Education and Loan Performance during a Housing Crisis." *American Economic Review*, vol. 100, no. 2 (May):495–500.

Banks, James, Cormac O'Dea, and Zoë Oldfield. 2010. "Cognitive Function, Numeracy and Retirement Saving Trajectories." *Economic Journal*, vol. 120, no. 548 (November):F381–F410.

Barber, Brad M., and Terrance Odean. 2001. "The Internet and the Investor." *Journal of Economic Perspectives*, vol. 15, no. 1 (Winter):41–54.

Baumeister, Roy F., Erin A. Sparks, Tyler F. Stillman, and Kathleen D. Vohs. 2008. "Free Will in Consumer Behavior: Self-Control, Ego Depletion, and Choice." *Journal of Consumer Psychology*, vol. 18, no. 1 (January):4–13.

Bell, Catherine J., Dan R. Gorin, and Jeanne M. Hogarth. 2009. "Does Financial Education Affect Soldiers' Financial Behavior?" Networks Financial Institute Working Paper No. 2009-08 (August).

Benartzi, Shlomo, and Richard H. Thaler. 2001. "Naive Diversification Strategies in Defined Contribution Savings Plans." *American Economic Review*, vol. 91, no. 1 (March):79–98.

Bettinger, Eric P., Bridget Terry Long, Philip Oreopoulos, and Lisa Sanbonmatsu. 2009. "The Role of Simplification and Information in College Decisions: Results from the H&R Block FAFSA Experiment." Working paper (September): https://cepa.stanford.edu/sites/default/files/Bettinger%20Long%20Oreopoulos%20Sanbonmatsu%20-%20FAFSA%20paper%201-22-12.pdf.

Braucher, Jean. 2001. "An Empirical Study of Debtor Education in Bankruptcy: Impact on Chapter 13 Completion Not Shown." *American Bankruptcy Institute Law Review* (Winter):557–592.

Brown, Amy, and Kimberly Gartner. 2007. "Early Intervention and Credit Cardholders: Results of Efforts to Provide Online Financial Education to New-to-Credit and At-Risk Consumers." Center for Financial Services Innovation (January): http://cfsinnovation.com/system/files/imported/managed_documents/earlyintervention.pdf.

Caplin, Andrew, and John Leahy. 2003. "Behavioral Policy." In *The Psychology of Economic Decisions: Volume I: Rationality and Well-Being*. Edited by Isabelle Brocas and Juan D. Carillo. New York: Oxford University Press.

Cesarini, David, Magnus Johannesson, Paul Lichtenstein, Örjan Sandewall, and Björn Wallace. 2010. "Genetic Variation in Financial Decision-Making." *Journal of Finance*, vol. 65, no. 5 (October):1725–1754.

Choi, James J., David Laibson, and Brigitte C. Madrian. 2010. "Why Does the Law of One Price Fail? An Experiment on Index Mutual Funds." *Review of Financial Studies*, vol. 23, no. 4 (April):1405–1432.

Choi, James J., David Laibson, Brigitte C. Madrian, and Andrew Metrick. 2001. "For Better or for Worse: Default Effects and 401(k) Savings Behavior." NBER Working Paper No. 8651 (December).

———. 2006. "Saving for Retirement on the Path of Least Resistance." In *Behavioral Public Finance*. Edited by Edward J. McCaffery and Joel Slemrod. New York: Russell Sage Foundation.

Cialdini, Robert B. 2001. *Influence: Science and Practice*. Needham Heights, MA: Allyn & Bacon.

Cole, Shawn, and Gauri Kartini Shastry. 2008. "If You Are So Smart, Why Aren't You Rich? The Effects of Education, Financial Literacy and Cognitive Ability on Financial Market Participation." Harvard Business School working paper (December).

De Neve, Jan-Emmanuel, and James H. Fowler. 2009. "The MAOA Gene Predicts Credit Card Debt." Working paper (August): http://polmeth.wustl.edu/media/Paper/maoa_and_credit_card_debt.pdf.

Gale, William G., and Ruth Levine. 2011. "Financial Literacy: What Works? How Could It Be More Effective?" Financial Security Project Working Paper 2011-1 (February).

Gallup. 2011. "Gallup Finds U.S. Unemployment Down to 9.4% in April" (5 May): http://www.gallup.com/poll/147428/gallup-finds-unemployment-down-april.aspx.

Garman, E. Thomas, Jinhee Kim, Constance Y. Kratzer, Bruce H. Brunson, and So-hyun Joo. 1999. "Workplace Financial Education Improves Personal Financial Wellness." *Financial Counseling and Planning*, vol. 10, no. 1:79–88.

Gerardi, Kristopher, Lorenz Goette, and Stephan Meier. 2010. "Financial Literacy and Subprime Mortgage Delinquency: Evidence from a Survey Matched to Administrative Data." Federal Reserve Bank of Atlanta Working Paper 2010-10 (April).

Hastings, Justine S., and Olivia S. Mitchell. 2011. "How Financial Literacy and Impatience Shape Retirement Wealth and Investment Behaviors." NBER Working Paper 16740 (January).

Hathaway, Ian, and Sameer Khatiwada. 2008. "Do Financial Education Programs Work?" Federal Reserve Bank of Cleveland Working Paper 2008-03.

Hershey, Douglas A., David A. Walsh, Ruby Brougham, Stephen Carter, and Alicia Farrell. 1998. "Challenges of Training Pre-Retirees to Make Sound Financial Planning Decisions." *Educational Gerontology*, vol. 24, no. 5:447–470.

Keinan, Giora. 1987. "Decision Making under Stress: Scanning of Alternatives under Controllable and Uncontrollable Threats." *Journal of Personality and Social Psychology*, vol. 52, no. 3 (March):639–644.

Lambert, Susan J., and Julia R. Henly. 2009. "Scheduling in Hourly Jobs: Promising Practices for the Twenty-First Century Economy." Mobility Agenda Policy Brief (May): http://www.mobilityagenda.org/home/page/Scheduling-in-Hourly-Jobs-Promising-Practices-for-the-Twenty-First-Century-Economy.aspx.

Lusardi, Annamaria, and Olivia S. Mitchell. 2009. "How Ordinary Consumers Make Complex Economic Decisions: Financial Literacy and Retirement Readiness." Paper presented at 11th Annual Joint Conference of the Retirement Research Consortium (10–11 August): http://www.nber.org/2009rrc/Summaries/2.1%20Lusardi,%20Mitchell.pdf.

Mallach, Alan. 2000. "Home Ownership Education and Counseling: Issues in Research and Definition." Federal Reserve Bank of Philadelphia Community Affairs Discussion Paper No. 00-01.

Mandell, Lewis. 2008. "Financial Literacy: Does It Matter?" In *Financial Literacy for Children and Youth.* Edited by Thomas A. Lucey and Kathleen S. Cooter. Athens, GA: Digitaltextbooks.biz.

Mandell, Lewis, and Linda Schmid Klein. 2009. "The Impact of Financial Literacy Education on Subsequent Financial Behavior." *Journal of Financial Counseling and Planning,* vol. 20, no. 1:15–24.

Maton, Cicily Carson, Michelle Maton, and William Marty Martin. 2010. "Collaborating with a Financial Therapist: The Why, Who, What, and How." *Journal of Financial Planning,* vol. 23, no. 2:62–70.

Meier, Stephan, and Charles Sprenger. 2007. "Selection into Financial Literacy Programs: Evidence from a Field Study." Federal Reserve Bank of Boston Public Policy Discussion Paper No. 07-5 (November).

Moore, Danna. 2003. "Survey of Financial Literacy in Washington State: Knowledge, Behavior, Attitudes, and Experiences." Washington State University Social and Economic Sciences Research Center Technical Report No. 03-39 (December).

National Association of Securities Dealers. 2006. "Investor Fraud Study Final Report." NASD Investor Education Foundation (May): http://www.finra.org/web/groups/foundation/@foundation/documents/foundation/p118422.pdf.

Pew Research Center for the People & the Press. 2009. "Trends in Political Values and Core Attitudes: 1987–2009." News release (May): http://people-press.org/files/legacy-pdf/517.pdf.

Quercia, Roberto G., and Susan M. Wachter. 1996. "Homeownership Counseling Performance: How Can It Be Measured?" *Housing Policy Debate,* vol. 7, no. 1:175–200.

Rasmussen, Carmen, and Jeffrey Bisanz. 2009. "Exploring Mathematics Difficulties in Children with Fetal Alcohol Spectrum Disorders." *Child Development Perspectives,* vol. 3, no. 2 (August):125–130.

Sethi-Iyengar, Sheena, Gur Huberman, and Wei Jiang. 2004. "How Much Choice Is Too Much? Contributions to 401(k) Retirement Plans." In *Pension Design and Structure: New Lessons from Behavioral Finance.* Edited by Olivia S. Mitchell and Stephen P. Utkus. New York: Oxford University Press.

Shiller, Robert J. 2006. "Long-Term Perspectives on the Current Boom in Home Prices."*Economists Voice,* vol. 3, no. 4.

Smith, James P., John J. McArdle, and Robert Willis. 2010. "Financial Decision Making and Cognition in a Family Context." *Economic Journal,* vol. 120, no. 548 (November):F363–F380.

Stephens, Melvin, Jr. 2004. "Job Loss Expectations, Realizations, and Household Consumption Behavior." *Review of Economics and Statistics*, vol. 86, no. 1 (February):253–269.

Taylor, H. Gerry, K.A. Espy, and P.J. Anderson. 2009. "Mathematics Deficiencies in Children with Very Low Birth Weight or Very Preterm Birth." *Developmental Disabilities Research Reviews*, vol. 15, no. 1:52–59.

Thaler, Richard H., and Shlomo Benartzi. 2004. "Save More Tomorrow: Using Behavioral Economics to Increase Employee Saving." *Journal of Political Economy*, vol. 112, no. S1 (February):S164–S187.

Trope, Yaacov, N. Liberman, and C. Wakslak. 2007. "Construal Levels and Psychological Distance: Effects on Representation, Prediction, Evaluation, and Behavior." *Journal of Consumer Psychology*, vol. 17, no. 2 (May):83–95.

U.S. GAO. 2006. "Credit Cards: Increased Complexity in Rates and Fees Heightens Need for More Effective Disclosures to Consumers." Report to the Ranking Minority Member, Permanent Subcommittee on Investigations, Committee on Homeland Security and Governmental Affairs, U.S. Senate (September): http://www.gao.gov/new.items/d06929.pdf.

van de Venter, Gerhard, and David Michayluk. 2008. "An Insight into Overconfidence in the Forecasting Abilities of Financial Advisors." *Australian Journal of Management*, vol. 32, no. 3 (March):545–557.

Vernick, Jon. S., Guohua Li, Susanne Ogaitis, Ellen J. MacKenzie, Susan P. Baker, and Andrea C. Gielen. 1999. "Effects of High School Driver Education on Motor Vehicle Crashes, Violations, and Licensure." *American Journal of Preventive Medicine*, vol. 16, no. 1: Supplement 1 (January):40–46.

Weinstein, Neil D. 1999. "What Does It Mean to Understand a Risk? Evaluating Risk Comprehension." *Journal of the National Cancer Institute*. Monographs, no. 25 (January):15–20.

Willis, Lauren E. 2008. "Against Financial Literacy Education." *Iowa Law Review*, vol. 94, no. 1:197–285.

———. 2009. "Evidence and Ideology in Assessing the Effectiveness of Financial Literacy Education." *San Diego Law Review*, vol. 46, no. 2 (May):415–458.

Session 6: Consumer Financial Protection and the Way Forward

Worry-Free Inflation-Indexing for Sovereigns: How Governments Can Effectively Deliver Inflation-Indexed Returns to Their Citizens and Retirees

Joseph Cherian[1]
Practice Professor of Finance
National University of Singapore

Wee Kang Chua
Research Analyst, Centre for Asset Management Research & Investments
National University of Singapore

Zvi Bodie
Norman and Adele Barron Professor of Management
Boston University School of Management

Retired people living on fixed incomes are more vulnerable to the risk of inflation than working people, whose incomes should, in theory, keep pace with inflation. Some governments currently offer citizens a way to protect themselves against inflation risk in old age, in the form of (1) automatic inflation-indexation of social security benefits or (2) the issuance of government-backed inflation-indexed bonds—for example, Treasury Inflation-Protected Securities (TIPS) in the United States, index-linked gilts in the United Kingdom, and so on.[2] Curiously, the governments of many Asian countries, which traditionally have cared deeply about the economic welfare of their population and provided social safety nets in a variety of ways for the most vulnerable

---

[1]Joseph Cherian presented this paper at the conference.

[2]In a recent comprehensive report titled "Global Aging Report (2010)," Standard & Poor's discusses how sovereigns will have to face the varying aging problems—and their adverse attendant costs to long-term public finances—in their respective regions.

members of society, do not offer any inflation-protected retirement benefits to their respective citizenry. Recent exceptions are Hong Kong and Thailand, which each issued an initial tranche of around US\$1.3 billion of inflation-linked bonds in July 2011. More recently, India and Singapore have expressed plans to study the introduction of inflation-linked bonds.

Government is the natural institution to provide inflation-linked benefits because tax revenues (both income and sales taxes) are indexed automatically to inflation. As observed in the sovereign debt crisis in Europe, however, the ability of small-country governments to guarantee inflation-proof income is limited. Nevertheless, new mechanisms for international risk transfer have developed in recent years. The rise of sovereign wealth funds, currency swap facilities between central banks, portfolio replication strategies, and the derivatives markets for credit default and CPI swaps have vastly expanded the scope for reallocating risk across various markets and nations. This has the potential effect of making the risk transfer process more efficient and transparent.

The average investor is concerned about three fundamental issues during retirement: (1) receiving a reasonable level payout every month that (2) lasts for as long as the investor lives and that (3) is indexed to his or her cost of living. In other words, an investor, upon retiring, would at a minimum like to receive a level *real* payout (i.e., one that is inflation indexed) for life that enables him to maintain his standard of living. The most commonly cited product that meets this need is an inflation-linked retirement annuity, which aims to convert accumulated investment capital to lifetime real cash flows for retirement consumption and expenditures.[3] Furthermore, the aging population and changing demographic landscape in such Asian countries as Japan, Hong Kong, Malaysia, and Singapore will serve to increase the demand for such retirement annuity products. In this respect, the lifelong income scheme (CPF LIFE) offered by the Central Provident Fund (CPF) in Singapore since 2009 took steps in the right direction to meet the first two criteria.[4] However, the monthly payouts in the various CPF LIFE plans do not have an inflation-indexing feature.

Taking a cue from investors in other economically developed nations, U.S., Japanese, Australian, and British investors will find that the simplest way to achieve a real, level payout for retirement spending purposes—apart from buying an inflation-linked retirement annuity—is to purchase a laddered portfolio of inflation-indexed bonds from their respective sovereign, with the first maturity of

---

[3]To this end, a U.S. company called Income Solutions (http://incomesolutions.com) has developed an indexed annuity delivery platform designed to enable transitioning U.S. employees in need of creating lifelong income to have online access to competitively bid, institutionally priced, immediate annuities (both inflation indexed and nominal).

[4]The CPF's monthly payouts are not strictly level but rather a function of the prevailing CPF interest rates and mortality experience. These parameters are reviewed annually and may be adjusted as often, albeit in a "smooth and stable" fashion.

the ladder occurring at retirement to finance that year's expenses and the final one at the expected mortality date, with some amount of hedging or insurance against longevity risk wrapped in.[5] Ideally, this laddered product would be purchased within a tax-deferred retirement program. If that option is not available, the investor could alternatively construct such a portfolio in a taxable investment account.

On the supply side, governments traditionally issue inflation-linked bonds so that investors, pension funds, insurance companies, and corporations can obtain inflation-indexed cash flows to meet their various liabilities and obligations that may grow with changes in CPI. Governments that issue inflation-indexed bonds include the United States (TIPS), United Kingdom (index-linked gilts), Japan (JGBi), France (OATi), Canada (RRBs), Sweden (SGILs), and Australia (CAINs). In a small number of cases, municipalities, utilities, and infrastructure funds, which receive inflation-indexed cash flows, have also been suppliers of indexed bonds, notes, and swaps.

A government faces two risks when issuing inflation-indexed bonds: the risk of the real interest rate going up and the risk of inflation rising. In both cases, it increases the government's cost of borrowing. The fiscal, monetary, and countercyclical tools usually available to a government enable it to somewhat control both risks. If all else fails, there are price controls, which some governments—such as Israel through its Economic Stabilization Policy—have successfully employed to suppress the runaway inflation of the 1970s and 1980s. Indeed, Israel's hyperinflation years saw its inflation rate spiral to a peak of 445% in 1984!

Singapore, too, has had its share of high CPI, albeit many orders of magnitude smaller than Israel's experience. In 1973, the annualized inflation rate in Singapore was 19.6%, followed by 22.3% the subsequent year. More recently, the Department of Statistics reported that Singapore's year-over-year inflation in September 2012 rose to 4.7%, reversing its slowing trend in the previous three months. This same CPI rate ranged between 5.5% and 7.5% in 2008. Being smaller, trade-based economies, Singapore and Israel are more susceptible to imported inflation as compared with the bigger economies, albeit the more recent inflation experience in Singapore has been demand-led, given rising transportation and housing costs. In such cases, countercyclical tools, such as currency appreciation, can also be used in an effective manner to manage inflation.

Although the issuance of sovereign inflation-indexed bonds is the most direct route to offer citizens the means to protect retirement income against inflation, we outline two other ways a small, trade-based country's government can provide inflation-indexed returns for retirement planning purposes. One is the use of derivatives, such as inflation swaps. Because derivatives are

---

[5]In the United States, the money manager PIMCO offers mutual fund products called Real Income Funds, which not only provide regular inflation-indexed distributions over time, as an annuity does, but also offer the liquidity inherent in open-end mutual funds.

usually unfunded or require only nominal margin collateral postings, such prescriptions enable a government to offer inflation-indexed returns without altering either its current portfolio of investments and economic activity or its monetary and fiscal policies. Another approach involves inflation-index replication strategies, which use a basket of correlated foreign inflation-linked bonds to broadly replicate the local inflation-indexed returns. The following section details the latter methodology. These methods allow governments to offer inflation-linked products to their citizens on a worry-free basis.

Manufacturing Inflation-Indexed Returns

In this section, we discuss the three ways in which a small (or "local") government can provide "risk-free" inflation hedging opportunities for its citizens. These recommendations are certainly not meant to be exhaustive. Indeed, innovations in the inflation-indexed business continue to yield many new forms of inflation hedging opportunities.

The first and most straightforward way of providing risk-free inflation hedging is for a government to issue inflation-indexed bonds. For example, the U.S. government issues TIPS, which are marketable securities whose face value (or principal) is adjusted by changes in the U.S. Consumer Price Index. TIPS pay interest semiannually and have maturities of 5, 10, and 30 years. Similarly, I Savings Bonds, another low-risk savings product from the U.S. government, earn an inflation-indexed interest rate on a tax-deferred, money market–type savings account.[6]

The second, and perhaps more creative, way of generating real returns at the sovereign level is via derivatives. As we mentioned earlier, because derivatives are usually unfunded, financial engineering technology enables a government to offer inflation-indexed bonds without altering either its current portfolio of investments and economic activity or its monetary and fiscal policies. We will not go into this methodology in great detail because there are a number of well-written industry guides on this topic. For an exhaustive description of the types of inflation-linked derivatives that are available in financial markets, please see Appendix B. There are, nevertheless, key elements in the methodology described in the third approach that can be beneficially ported to the extant derivatives technology available in the inflation-indexed industry.[7]

---

[6]The U.S. form of CPI is generally a short-hand for CPI-U, a price index that covers the out-of-pocket expenses of all urban consumers. In a recent working paper, Barnes, Bodie, Triest, and Wang (2009) provide evidence that TIPS indexed to CPI-U indeed provide hedges against unexpected changes in inflation for different types of U.S. investors because the various U.S. inflation measures are very highly correlated.

[7]Needless to say, there are numerous potential risks involved in this and other replicating technologies discussed here, including the default risk of the local government and/or of the governments whose bonds it might invest in. We address some of these issues in the next section of the paper.

The third suggested way to achieve this objective is for the local government to carve out a portion of its sovereign investment portfolio and invest it in a suitably weighted portfolio of other sovereigns' inflation-indexed bonds. For example, if Country A trades most with the United States, Australia, Japan, and the United Kingdom and the domestic demand for inflation-indexed bonds is US$1 billion, Government A can carve out a billion dollars of its sovereign wealth and invest in, say, a trade-weighted basket of U.S., Australian, Japanese, and U.K. inflation-indexed government securities.[8]

Theoretically, this weighted-average CPI replication methodology should succeed if strict purchasing power parity (PPP) holds. In that case, there would be no difference in real risk-free interest rates across markets. In reality, PPP does not hold, so the methodology will work only if the deviation from PPP is relatively small.

Table 1 summarizes the pros and cons of three proposed methods for manufacturing the local inflation index. The next section describes in greater detail our weighted-average inflation-index replication strategy.

Inflation-Index Replication

Preamble. The objective here is to assist small, trade-based countries, such as Singapore, in offering investors an investment product whose rate of return tracks the local inflation rate as measured by the local CPI. For this purpose, we construct a basket of liquid investable instruments whose returns track the CPI of a particular country as closely as possible. We refer to this as inflation-index replication.

The perspective we adopt here is that of an asset manager with a mandate to deliver returns at least equal to that of a target index's return but who has at his disposal only instruments that are imperfectly correlated with this index. Here, the target index is the local inflation index, and the imperfectly correlated instruments are the foreign inflation-indexed bonds. It is thus appropriate to use standard risk metrics and "performance" measures from the asset management industry to measure and quantify the "performance" of our inflation-index replication strategy. The industry standard measures we use include correlation, tracking error, alpha, information ratio, and the probability of shortfall.

There are many ways in which this inflation-index replication can be carried out. Choices include static or dynamic replication, where the components of the basket could be G–8 inflation-indexed bonds, commodity indices, and inflation-indexed exchange-traded funds. The weighting scheme used for the static or dynamically weighted basket could have as inputs the balance of

---

[8]In a recent research note similar to ours, Nomura's (2011) Fixed Income Research Department analyzed how Asian investors can use inflation instruments available in the U.S., European, and French markets and concluded that these instruments can help hedge Asian inflation.

Table 1.   Pros and Cons of Three Proposed Methods to Manufacture the Local Inflation Index

Method of Manufacturing Local Inflation Returns	Advantages	Risks	Mitigating Methods
Direct issuance of sovereign inflation-indexed bonds	• Simple, direct, exact • Government tax revenues and receipts rise naturally with inflation	• Sovereign bears full brunt of inflation risk • Taxable income and GDP may be adversely affected by inflation. Receipts might not rise sufficiently quickly	• Caps and floors on inflation payouts • Government has control over inflation via fiscal and monetary policies and price controls
Entering into inflation swaps	• Unfunded, requires minimal upfront capital • Sovereign bears minimal inflation risk	• Financial institution counterparty risk	• Direct sovereign or central bank–level swap arrangements
Replication using basket of correlated foreign inflation-indexed bonds	• Sovereign bears low to moderate residual inflation risk • Practical and feasible • Currency, interest rate, and default risk can be hedged	• Basket can sometimes underperform the local inflation index • Requires carving out of a portion of the sovereign investment portfolio • Hedging may be costly and/or impractical for the required time horizon	• Risk can be minimized by passing through the basket's returns directly to investors • Sovereign reserve and wealth portfolios usually already contain some foreign (especially G–3/G–7) bonds • Currency hedging via swaps can be directly arranged at the sovereign or central bank level

trade, housing indices, GDP, money supply, equity indices, and Organisation for Economic Co-Operation and Development leading indicators, with time horizons varying from short (1–2 years) to medium (3–5 years) to long term (10–30 years). Tracking accuracy normally would be measured as the absolute or squared deviation of average basket returns from the local CPIs.

The simplest strategy is to use 100% maturity-matched U.S. TIPS with the foreign currency exposure swapped out. *From 1971 to 2009, the U.S. annual inflation rate was below that of Singapore in only five years.* A more complex strategy is to form a portfolio of dynamically weighted and rebalanced G–8 inflation-indexed bonds to best match or optimize annual or maturity-matched inflation returns. The dynamic weighting scheme will be based on economic indicators, time horizon, expectations, and so on via systematic quantitative trading.

Needless to say, there are numerous potential pitfalls in attempting to replicate a local inflation index using a basket of foreign inflation-indexed bonds, which we will refer to as the "weighted-average CPI replication methodology." The first is model risk, given that historical CPI correlations or excess returns between countries may not hold in the future. It can be caused by changes in a country's reference inflation index. An example would be when the U.K. government switched from the Retail Prices Index (RPI) measure to the Consumer Prices Index (CPI) as its reference inflation index in 2010. The U.K. CPI is in general lower than the RPI; it was higher in only three months out of the last 20 years.

The second potential pitfall is "representativity" risk, which occurs when headline CPI understates actual price inflation for consumers on the ground. This is particularly pronounced in countries such as India, where recent headline CPI has been moderately high but actual food and fuel price increases have been much higher.

Third, currencies can be quite volatile, especially between the developed and developing markets. As a consequence, currency forward hedging over a horizon of more than a year is difficult and costly in terms of price spreads, especially for cross-currency hedges. And once the hedge is put on, it will likely be illiquid and difficult to unwind or adjust. Furthermore, for a small, trade-dependent country such as Singapore, which is susceptible to imported inflation, inflation will tend to spike when the local currency is weak. On the other hand, unhedged currency exposures could hurt if the foreign currency collapses because of a crisis. One way around the costly cross-currency hedging issue is for the sovereigns involved to enter bilateral or multilateral currency swap agreements using their respective central banks. In a way, this is a form of reinsurance of national default risk across transnational borders, because the government-to-government currency swap is essentially a credit default swap. There is, hence, a unique role for the government in this process as the reinsurer of last resort.

The fourth risk is interest rate risk. Interest rates can fluctuate, which, in turn, causes the prices of bonds to fluctuate because the prices of inflation-indexed bonds are determined by both interest rates and inflation expectations. Finally, sovereign risk in the form of sovereign defaults may become significant, as evidenced by events in Europe in early 2010. Icelandic and Greek sovereign bonds would have caused much grief for their investors. This risk can be mitigated somewhat by (1) avoiding bonds of weak or debt-ridden sovereigns when forming the inflation-index replication strategy and (2) sticking mainly to high-grade sovereigns, such as the G–8, which have low sovereign default risk.

Quantitative Methodology. For our analysis, we assume that currency risk, interest rate risk, and sovereign default risk can be hedged out for a low or negligible cost. This assumption takes care of Points 3 through 5 in the pitfalls mentioned earlier. Also, because our objective is simply the replication of the local CPI index returns, we need not concern ourselves with Point 2. That leaves us with only model risk, which is a risk that is inherent in any quantitative model. The adverse effects on our model from changes or adjustments in the reference inflation index should be low because local measures of inflation tend to be highly correlated.

We take the universe of countries with an investable inflation-indexed bond market of sufficient depth and liquidity to be the United States, the United Kingdom, France, Europe, Canada, Japan, and Sweden (hereafter referred to as "the universe"). We then examine inflation rates in Singapore, Malaysia, Taiwan, and Hong Kong (hereafter referred to as "countries of interest") with respect to the investable universe. For each country of interest, we look at the longest overlapping period of reported headline consumer price index data between that country and each country in the investable universe.[9] We then calculate the monthly, quarterly, and yearly CPI returns of that country up to December 2009 and use this result as a benchmark.[10] We then consider the historical performance of each country in the investable universe with respect to this benchmark. We also calculate various "performance" metrics, such as the mean alpha or "excess returns," tracking error, information ratio, historical shortfall, and correlation, and compare these with the benchmark.

This weighted-average CPI replication methodology approach has merit based on the notion that as long as there are free capital flows globally (or at least for the economies under consideration), and assuming purchasing power parity holds, there will be no difference in real risk-free rates across markets because differences in interest rates reflect differences in expected inflation. In Appendix C, we prove that this weighted-average CPI methodology is a sound one by starting with the PPP relationship. We go on to demonstrate that asset price changes in local terms are the same as asset price changes in foreign terms if there is no change in exchange rates or if exchange rates are fully hedged using currency swaps, forwards, or futures. As mentioned previously, however, PPP does not hold in reality, and hence the methodology will work only if deviations from PPP are moderate. We will next examine some strategies that

---

[9]Country CPI data are obtained from Thomson Reuters Datastream.

[10]We found that monthly and even quarterly data were too volatile, so we focus only on yearly data. Returns and excess returns are calculated on a continuously compounded annualized basis.

are middle-of-the-road in the complexity spectrum. The historical performance statistics of simple replication strategies, such as a portfolio consisting of 100% U.S. TIPS, are readily apparent when calculating the benchmarks.

Results and Discussion

In this section, we compare the performance of CPIs of countries in the investable universe with those of the various countries of interest (the benchmark) using such measures as the mean alpha or excess return, tracking error, information ratio, historical shortfall, and correlation. Our justification for using such measures is that our experiment is no different from an asset manager who has a mandate to deliver returns at least equal to that of a target index's return but who has only instruments that are imperfectly correlated with this index available at his disposal.

When comparing the performance of CPIs of countries in the investable universe against Singapore's CPI, **Table 2**, Panel A, indicates that the United Kingdom has the longest period, highest excess returns, highest information ratio, and lowest historical shortfall. Nevertheless, it also has the lowest correlation and the worst tracking error compared with Singapore. Meanwhile, Japan has nearly exactly the opposite characteristics. It has the lowest (even negative) alpha and the worst (negative) information ratio and historical shortfall but the highest correlation.

Even though a high correlation is desirable, the United States and the United Kingdom have the most liquid inflation-indexed markets compared with Japan's. Furthermore, the United States has the third-best correlation at 0.54, just below Canada. The United States also has the second-best historical shortfall. Japan's historical shortfall percentage is too high because of the poor mean alpha caused by deflation.

As a consequence, it is our view that a combination of U.S. and U.K. CPI will be able to best improve correlation and tracking error, with the least effect on historical shortfall and information ratio.

For Malaysia (Table 2, Panel B), once again the U.K. indexed bonds have the best excess returns, highest information ratio, and lowest historical shortfall. But they also have the worst tracking error. Best tracking error goes to Europe, with France a close second. Best correlation goes to Japan, with the United States and Canada tied for second place, and the United States edges out Canada for tracking error, information ratio, and historical shortfall. Thus, the United States is a very good addition to the portfolio to boost the overall correlation, with the least adverse impact on the other metrics.

Table 2. Performance of CPIs of Countries in Investable Universe Compared with CPI of Singapore, Malaysia, Taiwan, and Hong Kong

Country	Start	End	Period Length	Mean Alpha (%)	Tracking Error (%)	Information Ratio	Historical Shortfall (%)	Correlation
A. Singapore								
U.S.	Dec 1961	Dec 2009	48 yrs.	1.52	3.89	0.42	18.8	0.54
U.K.	Dec 1961	Dec 2009	48 yrs.	3.25	5.97	0.64	10.4	0.36
France	Dec 1990	Dec 2009	19 yrs.	0.06	1.42	0.04	36.8	0.39
Europe	Dec 1996	Dec 2009	13 yrs.	0.62	1.67	0.38	23.1	0.45
Canada	Dec 1961	Dec 2009	48 yrs.	1.55	3.92	0.43	20.8	0.55
Japan	Dec 1970	Dec 2009	39 yrs.	−0.13	3.32	−0.04	61.5	0.72
Sweden	Dec 1961	Dec 2009	48 yrs.	2.31	4.96	0.52	27.1	0.36
B. Malaysia								
U.S.	Dec 1972	Dec 2009	37 yrs.	0.68	2.81	0.25	35.1	0.59
U.K.	Dec 1972	Dec 2009	37 yrs.	2.43	5.27	0.51	32.4	0.42
France	Dec 1990	Dec 2009	19 yrs.	−1.26	1.87	−0.89	73.7	−0.08
Europe	Dec 1996	Dec 2009	13 yrs.	−0.60	1.64	−0.38	61.5	−0.35
Canada	Dec 1972	Dec 2009	37 yrs.	0.70	2.96	0.24	37.8	0.59
Japan	Dec 1972	Dec 2009	37 yrs.	−1.08	2.94	−0.39	75.7	0.79
Sweden	Dec 1972	Dec 2009	37 yrs.	1.23	3.99	0.32	40.5	0.41
C. Taiwan								
U.S.	Dec 1959	Dec 2009	50 yrs.	−0.20	4.51	−0.04	34.0	0.69
U.K.	Dec 1959	Dec 2009	50 yrs.	1.55	5.57	0.29	26.0	0.51
France	Dec 1990	Dec 2009	19 yrs.	−0.19	1.46	−0.12	57.9	0.50
Europe	Dec 1996	Dec 2009	13 yrs.	0.91	1.48	0.75	15.4	0.37
Canada	Dec 1959	Dec 2009	50 yrs.	−0.18	4.79	−0.04	42.0	0.60
Japan	Dec 1970	Dec 2009	39 yrs.	−1.36	3.91	−0.37	71.8	0.82
Sweden	Dec 1959	Dec 2009	50 yrs.	0.64	5.35	0.12	40.0	0.47
D. Hong Kong								
U.S.	Dec 1980	Dec 2009	29 yrs.	−1.36	4.29	−0.33	58.6	0.57
U.K.	Dec 1980	Dec 2009	29 yrs.	−0.60	3.79	−0.16	58.6	0.63
France	Dec 1990	Dec 2009	19 yrs.	−1.11	4.40	−0.25	57.9	0.40
Europe	Dec 1996	Dec 2009	13 yrs.	1.74	3.24	0.61	38.5	0.06
Canada	Dec 1980	Dec 2009	29 yrs.	−1.38	4.33	−0.33	65.5	0.51
Japan	Dec 1980	Dec 2009	29 yrs.	−3.70	5.30	−0.95	79.3	0.79
Sweden	Dec 1980	Dec 2009	29 yrs.	−0.89	3.52	−0.26	72.4	0.70

Notes: Light gray highlights denote the best metrics for each category. Dark gray highlights denote the worst.

As Table 2, Panel C, indicates, for Taiwan, the U.K. CPI has the highest mean alpha and also the best information ratio and historical shortfall outside of Europe. It has the worst tracking error. Japan still has the worst alpha, information ratio, and historical shortfall. To boost correlation, one can add a U.S. component, which has the second-highest correlation after Japan.

It turned out to be very challenging to replicate and outperform Hong Kong's CPI (see Table 2, Panel D). Europe has the best alpha, tracking error, information ratio, and historical shortfall but the worst correlation, and Japan has exactly the opposite result, with a negative alpha that is of a much larger magnitude than Europe's positive alpha. The United Kingdom and Sweden are the best candidates to boost correlation without decreasing alpha too badly. Compared with Sweden, the United Kingdom is superior in terms of mean alpha, information ratio, and historical shortfall, while losing out in terms of tracking error and correlation.

The boxplot in **Figure 1** graphs the summary CPI statistics for various countries and regions. It includes the median, 25th and 75th percentiles, minima and maxima, and also outliers, defined as data points that are 1.5 times the interquartile range beyond either quartile, as individual points. The boxplot ranges for Europe and France are much smaller than those for the other countries because the HICP data (on which the inflation indexed bonds are based) have a shorter history.

Figure 1. Summary CPI Statistics for Various Countries/Regions

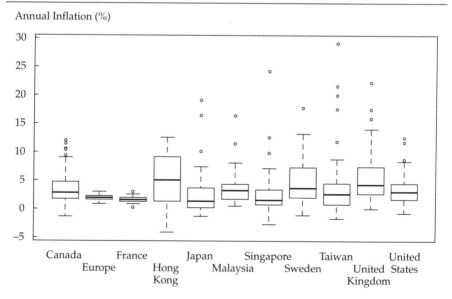

Table 3 provides the summary statistics, such as mean, standard deviation, minima, maxima, and 25th and 75th percentiles, of the CPI for all countries of interest.

Table 4 shows the correlations between the year-over-year percentage change in inflation index for countries of interest.

Correlations between the year-over-year percentage change in inflation index of countries of interest are shown as a heat map in **Figure 2**: The darker the gray hue, the higher the correlation. Additionally, countries are grouped into clusters or cliques by correlation, with countries in the same cluster having the highest correlations. Asian countries have high cross-correlation with each other, and the Western countries form another clique. Asia further breaks down into Singapore, Malaysia, and Taiwan against Hong Kong and Japan. Malaysia and Taiwan form the smallest grouping. This result makes sense because they have similar profiles, both being emerging economies with a high-tech/industrial sector as well as a large agricultural sector. The

Figure 2.   Heat Map of Year-over-Year CPI Change for Various Countries/Regions

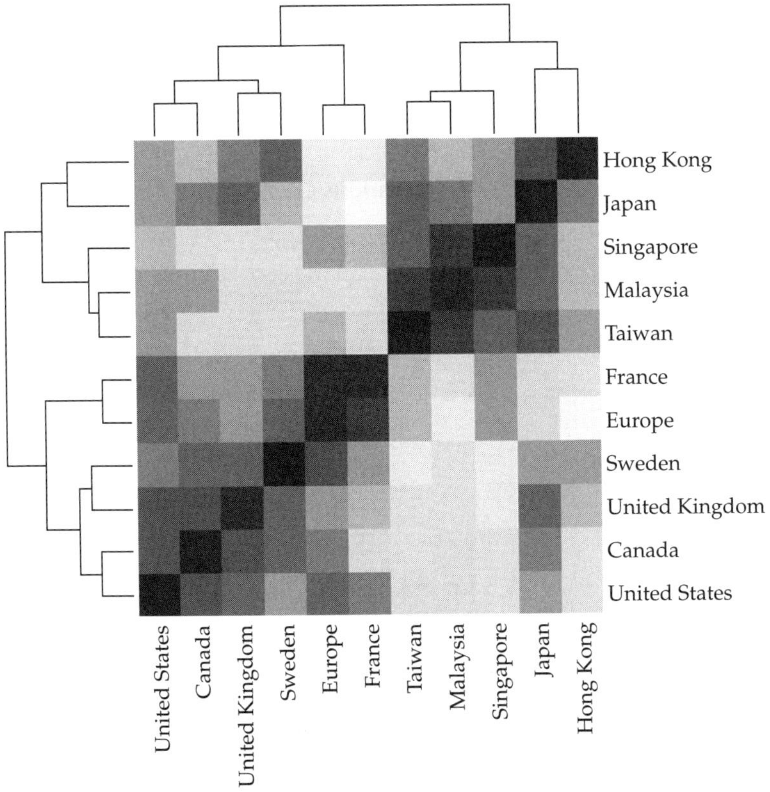

Table 3. Summary CPI Statistics for Various Countries/Regions

	United States	United Kingdom	Japan	Canada	Sweden	France	Europe	Singapore	Malaysia	Taiwan	Hong Kong
Mean	3.7%	5.5%	2.8%	3.7%	4.8%	1.6%	1.8%	2.6%	3.7%	4.2%	4.5%
Standard deviation	2.8	4.6	4.4	3.2	3.8	0.6	0.6	4.3	3.1	6.0	4.8
Min.	-0.7	0.0	-1.3	-1.4	-1.1	0.2	0.7	-2.8	0.5	-1.7	-4.1
25th percentile	1.7	2.6	0.1	1.6	1.9	1.2	1.5	0.7	1.7	0.8	1.3
Median	3.0	4.3	1.4	2.8	3.7	1.6	1.8	1.5	3.2	2.6	5.1
75th percentile	4.3	7.2	3.5	4.6	7.2	1.9	2.1	3.3	4.2	4.4	9.0
Max.	12.5	22.2	19.1	11.9	17.8	2.9	3.0	24.1	16.4	29.2	12.6

Table 4. Correlation of Year-over-Year CPI Change for Various Countries/Regions

	Singapore	United States	United Kingdom	France	Europe	Canada	Japan	Sweden	Malaysia	Taiwan	Hong Kong
Singapore	1.00	0.55	0.38	0.55	0.62	0.49	0.71	0.38	0.86	0.75	0.51
United States	0.55	1.00	0.83	0.75	0.82	0.87	0.71	0.69	0.61	0.60	0.55
United Kingdom	0.38	0.83	1.00	0.55	0.62	0.81	0.79	0.77	0.45	0.46	0.60
France	0.55	0.75	0.55	1.00	0.96	0.54	0.39	0.65	0.31	0.49	0.29
Europe	0.62	0.82	0.62	0.96	1.00	0.70	0.48	0.82	0.33	0.53	0.23
Canada	0.49	0.87	0.81	0.54	0.70	1.00	0.72	0.77	0.55	0.50	0.47
Japan	0.71	0.71	0.79	0.39	0.48	0.72	1.00	0.64	0.74	0.78	0.75
Sweden	0.38	0.69	0.77	0.65	0.82	0.77	0.64	1.00	0.43	0.41	0.66
Malaysia	0.86	0.61	0.45	0.31	0.33	0.55	0.74	0.43	1.00	0.86	0.50
Taiwan	0.75	0.60	0.46	0.49	0.53	0.50	0.78	0.41	0.86	1.00	0.59
Hong Kong	0.51	0.55	0.60	0.29	0.23	0.47	0.75	0.66	0.50	0.59	1.00

West breaks down into the pairs France and Europe, the United Kingdom and Sweden, and the United States and Canada. Interestingly, Sweden and the United Kingdom are grouped into the same clique with Canada and the United States, instead of France and Europe.

From the annual CPI percentage change of the G–3 countries illustrated in **Figure 3**, we can see that their inflation changes are highly correlated. In addition, we also observe peaks in inflation in both the early and late 1970s.

From **Figure 4**, we notice that inflation in the small, trade-dependent Asian countries (Singapore, Malaysia, and Taiwan, in particular) is also quite highly correlated, with peaks in the 1970s. Hong Kong has a wider variation of inflation from the 1980s to the early 2000s but has recently had inflation that is very correlated with its other small, trade-dependent Asian counterparts.

We also observe in **Figure 5** that the annual U.K. RPI has, in general, "out-performed" the CPI of the Asian trade-dependent sovereigns except for a brief period in the early 1970s and also in the 1980s to mid-1990s for Hong Kong.

Figure 6 illustrates how various combinations of U.S. and U.K. infla-tion-indexed bonds would have performed with respect to Singapore's infla-tion index. A portfolio consisting of between 20% and 30% U.K. inflation-indexed bonds, with the remainder in U.S. inflation-indexed bonds, would have been optimal in terms of *ex post* information ratio, shortfall probability, shortfall occurrences, and excess return. This finding is in line with the proof in Appendix C that a weighted combination of major inflation indices is a sensible hedge for local inflation.

Figure 3. Annual CPI Percentage Change of the G–3 Countries

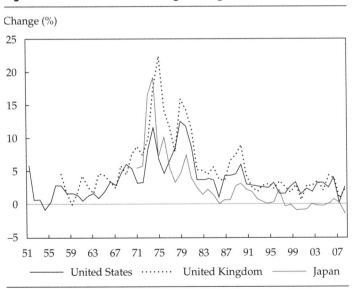

Figure 4. **Annual CPI Percentage Change of Trade-Dependent Sovereigns**

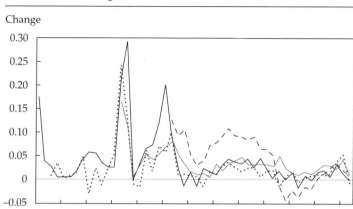

Figure 5. **Outperformance of U.K. CPI against Sovereigns' CPI** (percentage change)

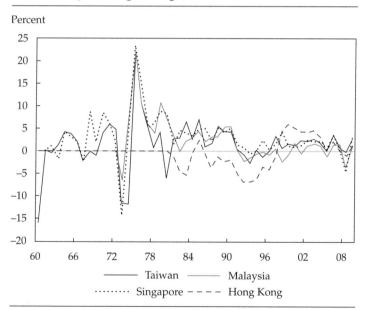

Figure 6. Outperformance of Various Weighted Combinations of U.S. and U.K. CPI against Singapore CPI
(percentage change)

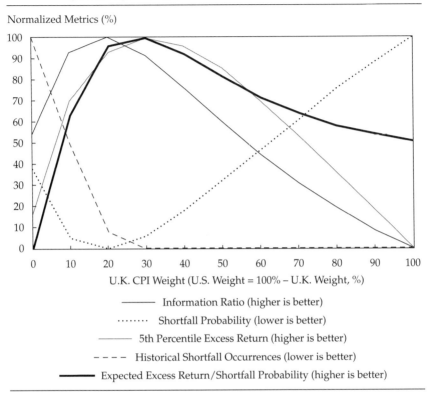

Normalized Metrics (%)

U.K. CPI Weight (U.S. Weight = 100% − U.K. Weight, %)

——— Information Ratio (higher is better)

········· Shortfall Probability (lower is better)

·—·—· 5th Percentile Excess Return (higher is better)

– – – Historical Shortfall Occurrences (lower is better)

▬▬▬ Expected Excess Return/Shortfall Probability (higher is better)

Conclusion

We have discussed three methods by which small countries, such as Malaysia, Singapore, and Taiwan, can use financial tools to offer their aging populations the means to protect retirement income against inflation. The first method is the direct issuance of inflation-indexed bonds. The second method is through the use of inflation swaps. The third method is to invest in a basket of foreign inflation-indexed bonds with stable and sufficient correlation with the local inflation index, while hedging out currency and interest rate risks. The last two methods have the benefit of not requiring governments to directly issue inflation-indexed bonds.

Our analysis indicates that a broad-based weighted-average CPI replication measure has merit in hedging inflation risk. Indeed, assuming PPP holds and that there are free capital flows globally, there will be no difference in real risk-free rates across markets because differences in interest rates reflect differences in expected inflation.

Using simple performance and risk metrics utilized in portfolio management, we find that in most cases, a combination of U.S., Japanese, and U.K. inflation-indexed bonds is sufficient to replicate and hedge the local inflations of Singapore, Malaysia, Hong Kong, and Taiwan. This finding is not unexpected because the annual CPI percentage changes of the G–3 countries (the United States, Japan, and the United Kingdom) are highly correlated, whereas inflation rates in the smaller, trade-dependent Asian countries, such as Singapore, Malaysia, and Taiwan, also are highly correlated.

With this ability to provide inflation-adjusted returns, governments, pension funds, and other institutions can begin to offer a broad suite of inflation-indexed products, ranging from retirement annuities to inflation-linked insurance policies. Such offerings will improve the functioning of national pension systems and, hence, the welfare of retirees. The added benefit of such structures is that they allow governments to broadly replicate their local CPI returns without disrupting their traditional financing structures.

Finally, given the potential of reinsuring national default risks across borders via currency and credit default swap facilities at the federal level, there is also a unique role for the government during this process to serve as the reinsurer of last resort.

Appendix A. Countries Issuing Inflation-Indexed Bonds

The tables in this appendix are reproduced from "Experiences in Japan: Inflation Indexed Bond Markets," Yukinobu Kitamura, Hitotsubashi University working paper (30 January 2009).

Exhibit A1. Countries Issuing Inflation-Indexed Bonds

Country	Issue Date	Index Used
Argentina	1972–89	Non-agriculture wholesale price
Australia	1983–	Consumer prices
	1991	Average weekly earnings
Austria	1953	Electricity prices
Brazil	1964–90	Wholesale prices
	1991–	General prices
Canada	1991–	Consumer prices
Chile	1966–	Consumer prices
Colombia	1967	Wholesale prices
	1995–	Consumer prices
Czech Republic	1997–	Consumer prices

(continued)

Exhibit A1. Countries Issuing Inflation-Indexed Bonds (continued)

Country	Issue Date	Index Used
Denmark	1982–	Consumer prices
Finland	1945–67	Wholesale prices
France	1952, 1973	Gold price
	1956	Level of industrial production
	1956	Average value of French securities
	1957	Price of equities
Greece	1997–	Consumer prices
Hungary	1995–	Consumer prices
Iceland	1955–	Consumer prices
	1964–80	Cost of building index
	1980–94	Credit terms index
	1995–	Consumer prices
Ireland	1983–	Consumer prices
Israel	1955–	Consumer prices
Italy	1983	Deflator of GDP at factor cost
Mexico	1989–	Consumer prices
New Zealand	1977–84	Consumer prices
	1995	Consumer prices
Norway	1982	Consumer prices
Poland	1992–	Consumer prices
Sweden	1952	Consumer prices
	1994–	Consumer prices
Turkey	1994–97	Wholesale prices
	1997–	Consumer prices
United Kingdom	1975–	Consumer prices
	1981–	Consumer prices
United States	1742, 1780	Commodity prices
	1997–	Consumer prices

Note: In addition to government bonds, this table includes issues by public corporations, semi-government authorities, and those that carry a government guarantee.
Sources: Mark Deacon and Andrew Derry, *Inflation-Indexed Securities* (New York: Prentice Hall 1998). Table 1.1, page 6. (Reproduced from Table 1, page 8, in Yukinobu Kitamura, "Experiences in Japan: Inflation Indexed Bond Markets," Hitotsubashi University working paper, 30 January 2009).

Size of Issuance:

> United States: $536.2 billion as of October 2008
> United Kingdom: £157 billion as of September 2008
> France: €151.3 billion as of September 2008
> Italy: €83.7 billion as of October 2008
> Canada: C$31.5 billion as of November 2008
> Japan: ¥1,010 billion as of December 2008

Sources: Treasury Department of the United States, Debt Management Office of United Kingdom, the Department of Treasury of Italy, Bank of Canada, Ministry of Finance of Japan, and the Bank of Japan (Mizuho Securities). Reproduced from Table 2, page 9 in Yukinobu Kitamura, "Experiences in Japan: Inflation Indexed Bond Markets," Hitotsubashi University working paper (30 January 2009).

Appendix B. Using Derivatives to Hedge Inflation Risk

Types of Contracts. Reproduced from Barclay's Capital (formerly Lehman Brothers) Fixed Income Research Department's Interest Rate Strategy article, "Inflation Derivatives: An Intuitive Approach," 23 June 2008. Products and definitions are excerpted directly from the Lehman article.

1. **Zero-Coupon Inflation Swaps.** In a zero-coupon swap, the buyer receives the cumulative inflation payment at expiry of the contract and does not receive any income over and above the inflation rate. The contract, therefore, directly trades inflation, not real yields. More specifically, a zero-coupon inflation swap is a bilateral contract in which, at termination, the inflation buyer (receiver) pays a predetermined fixed rate (a.k.a. the "inflation break-even rate") and receives the cumulative change in the CPI index from the inflation payer (seller). There is no exchange of cash flows at inception or during the life of the contract (other than collateral postings).

2. **Price Index Swaps.** A price index swap, or a "revenue swap," is similar to a zero-coupon inflation swap, with the difference being that it has periodic (typically annual) cash flows. At each payment date, the inflation receiver pays the pre-agreed fixed inflation breakeven rate in exchange for the overall change in CPI since inception.

3. **OTC Inflation Bond/Real Yield Swap.** An OTC inflation bond, or a real yield swap, is a contract in which a party receives a real interest rate (i.e., a "real" coupon that accretes at the rate of realized inflation in exchange for LIBOR floating rate payments). To mimic TIPS cash flows, the real rate in the United States is typically quoted semiannually versus quarterly LIBOR payments. And, as with TIPS, at maturity the real rate receiver pays par

and receives an inflation-adjusted principal (or simply receives the inflation uplift). The real coupon rate is determined by the implied expected nominal cash flows on the inflation leg being projected using the inflation curve against the floating LIBOR payments, both discounted at LIBOR flat. The real coupon is then solved for, such that the NPV of the floating leg matches that of the real rate leg (so that the swap has zero value at onset).

4. **Inflation Asset Swaps.** An inflation asset swap involves purchasing an inflation bond (e.g., a TIPS) and then passing on all its cash flows to the asset swap seller in exchange for LIBOR ± spread. At maturity, the buyer pays the inflation-adjusted principal it receives from the TIPS, in return for par or the market price. Note, unlike the earlier instruments discussed, the buyer of the inflation asset swap does not have any inflation or real rate exposure. The asset swap buyer simply passes on the cash flows it receives from the TIPS held on the balance sheet to the asset swap seller in exchange of LIBOR ± spread. The only exposure the asset swap buyer has is to the spread to LIBOR, which is commonly referred to as the "asset swap spread" (ASW).

5. Finally, **Inflation Futures (CME)** and **Inflation Options (OTC)** also exist.

Challenges

*   There is currently a low level of liquidity and issuance in both the global inflation-indexed bond markets as well as the inflation-indexed derivatives markets.

*   Basis risk.

Inflation-Linked Sovereign Swaps: How It Would Work

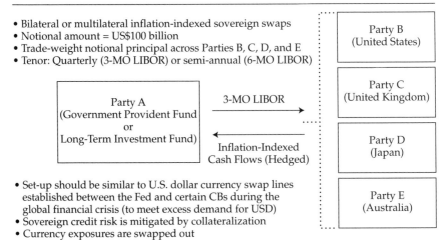

Appendix C. Proof of the Weighted-Average CPI Methodology Starting from the PPP Relationship

We show here that the asset price change in local terms is the same as the asset price change in foreign terms if there is either

1. No change in exchange rates, or

2. Exchange rates are fully hedged using forwards or futures.

Let A be the price of a particular basket of goods/assets in local currency terms and B be the price of the exact same basket in foreign currency terms. Let subscripts denote the discrete times at which we are observing the asset prices. Let S be currency exchange rate in amount of local currency per unit of foreign currency.

Assuming purchasing power parity (PPP), we have

$$A_t = B_t S_t.$$

It follows that

$$\frac{A_{t+1}}{A_t} = \frac{B_{t+1} S_{t+1}}{B_t S_t},$$

and clearly

$$\frac{A_{t+1}}{A_t} = \frac{B_{t+1}}{B_t},$$

if S stays the same at two time instants. If we take the basket to be a reference basket of goods, this shows that under the PPP assumption, the fractional CPI change in one country should be the same as the fractional CPI change in another if exchange rates do not fluctuate.

Now, of course, in the real world, exchange rates do not stay constant. In fact, they fluctuate wildly. Let's examine what happens when we hedge out the fluctuations in exchange rates using a forward exchange contract. Let F_t denote the forward exchange rate at time t.

At the initial time t, our foreign basket of goods would be worth in local terms

$$A_t = B_t S_t.$$

At the next time instant $t + 1$, our currency-hedged basket of goods would be worth in local terms

$$A_{t+1} = B_{t+1} S_{t+1} + \left(F_t - S_{t+1} \right) B_t,$$

where the second term is the profit or loss caused by the forward contract hedge on the starting foreign currency amount. Hence, our return in local asset terms is

$$\frac{A_{t+1}}{A_t} = \frac{B_{t+1}S_{t+1} + (F_t - S_{t+1})B_t}{B_t S_t}.$$

Factoring out $\dfrac{B_{t+1}}{B_t}$ from the right-hand side, we obtain

$$\frac{A_{t+1}}{A_t} = \frac{B_{t+1}}{B_t}\left[\frac{S_{t+1}}{S_t} + \left(\frac{F_t}{S_t} - \frac{S_{t+1}}{S_t}\right)\frac{B_t}{B_{t+1}}\right].$$

If the time interval is short, $\dfrac{F_t}{S_t} \approx 1$ as forward prices will not be far from spot and $\dfrac{B_t}{B_{t+1}} \approx 1$ if we have a reasonable rate of inflation in foreign terms. Hence,

$$\frac{A_{t+1}}{A_t} \approx \frac{B_{t+1}}{B_t}\left[\frac{S_{t+1}}{S_t} + \left(1 - \frac{S_{t+1}}{S_t}\right)\right] = \frac{B_{t+1}}{B_t},$$

or

$$\frac{A_{t+1}}{A_t} \approx \frac{B_{t+1}}{B_t},$$

regardless of how much the spot price ratio $\dfrac{S_{t+1}}{S_t}$ has changed.

We now add in more foreign countries, Bi. Let $\Delta CPI_{country} \equiv \log country_{t+1}/country_t$ denote the continuously compounded change in CPI levels for a country. Then we have

$$\Delta CPI_{local} = \Delta CPI_{foreign,i}$$
$$w_i\Delta CPI_{local} = w_i\Delta CPI_{foreign,i}$$
$$\Delta CPI_{local} = \sum_i w_i\Delta CPI_{foreign,i},$$

where w_i represents the weights that sum to 1.

REFERENCES

Barclays Capital. 2008. "Inflation Derivatives: An Intuitive Approach." Fixed Income Research Department's Interest Rate Strategy article (23 June).

Barnes, Michelle L., Zvi Bodie, Robert K. Triest, and J. Christina Wang. 2009. "A TIPS Scorecard: Are TIPS Accomplishing What They Were Supposed to Accomplish? Can They Be Improved?" Federal Reserve Bank Public Policy Discussion Paper No. 09–8.

Deacon, Mark, and Andrew Derry. 1998. *Inflation-Indexed Securities*. New York: Prentice Hall.

Kitamura, Yukinobu. 2009. "Experiences in Japan: Inflation Indexed Bond Markets." Hitotsubashi University working paper (30 January).

Nomura Fixed Income, Currency and Commodities Division. 2011. "Think Global: How to Hedge Asian Inflation." Fixed Income Research Department's Inflation Strategy article (19 April).

Session 6: Consumer Financial Protection and the Way Forward

Discussion

David Buchholz, Moderator
Manager of Policy Analysis
Federal Reserve Board

Tamar Frankel
Professor
Boston University School of Law

David Weil
Everett W. Lord Distinguished Faculty Scholar
Boston University School of Management

Henriette Prast
Professor
Tilburg University

Tamar Frankel

In addition to teaching investors *how* to invest, we should be teaching them *whom* to go to for advice. In other words, rather than trying to make investors experts in a complicated field, we should be helping them identify who the experts are and what they should ask them.

Learning to Be a Proficient Customer. It is inefficient to teach everyone to be a professional investor, just as it is inefficient to try to turn everyone into their own doctor, lawyer, plumber, or car mechanic. After all, those professions provide an array of recognized experts who provide attestable expertise. Investment management is a field that could benefit from this model.

The worst outcome occurs when people ask each other for investment advice. This creates a herding effect that can lead directly to the success of con artists and Ponzi schemes. What people need is a reliable way of identifying genuine experts.

If people do not know enough about investing, then they need help from an expert. And when they invest through such experts, they are transferring a certain amount of control over their financial assets. They are placing great trust in somebody else. This model creates risks because these "somebodies" (no matter what their fiduciary role may be) can be tempted to mismanage the financial assets entrusted to them, which is the reason we have rules governing people who are entrusted with power over other people's assets. And that leads me to regulation.[1]

Sensible Regulation and Investor Education. At this conference, I have heard some mention of regulation—not much, but some—and what I heard has not had an approving tone. But because I am suggesting that people should ask others for advice, then those providing the advice should be governed by certain rules. When I give a broker my money to invest, I may be told not to trust that person. But, of course, I will trust that person. Our relationship requires it. If that person gives me advice, I may have to accept that advice; otherwise, the relationship does not work. It does not make sense to give someone all of my savings to invest for me and then reject his or her investment advice. And research has demonstrated that people do trust their financial brokers and advisers. Unfortunately, too many brokers and advisers view themselves as salespeople only.

Many brokers speak about performing their services with care. They speak of giving their clients the expertise of their advice. But I am talking about more than that. I am talking about loyalty, which is an entirely different concept. Brokers are responsible for money that has never been theirs and never will be theirs, and the advice they provide is based on a power given to them in trust by their customers. Yet many brokers do not want to acknowledge the level of power they have accepted. My response is that if they do not want such power, they should not offer advice. Let them perform their functions as brokers and leave it at that. Yet even with respect to those functions, brokers take on fiduciary responsibilities, whether they want to or not. They are trustees; they hold other people's money.

However, because we are unlikely to have regulations that will impose such duties on brokers and other similar market intermediaries, I suggest that we at least teach investors to ask the right questions. We can give them a simple summary of Form ADV under the Investment Advisers Act of 1940 so that they can ask their chosen experts 12–15 essential questions, such as the following:

- How much do you charge me?

- Who pays you for selling, in addition to me?

- Can the investment you are recommending be obtained more cheaply somewhere else?

---

[1]See Tamar Frankel, *Fiduciary Law* (Oxford, U.K.: Oxford University Press, 2006).

Investors should ask their advisers to fill a form with their answers to those 12–15 questions and sign it. The investors should keep a copy. The advisers should keep a copy. That way, investors may be better protected from advice that is truly sales-talk.

David Weil

In the tradition of academic institutions, I have had a series of hallway discussions about the topic of disclosure and the impact of disclosure on some of the issues we have discussed at this conference. In that respect, I would like to address three questions about the efficacy of disclosure.

- Does disclosure provide any opportunity for addressing the issues raised in the panel on financial education?

- What are the differences between effective and ineffective disclosure policies?

- Can we do a better job through the use of disclosure?

Effective and Ineffective Disclosure. As co-director of the Transparency Policy Project at the Kennedy School, I have spent a number of years examining a wide range of disclosure policies (financial and nonfinancial), many of which are intended to remedy the type of problems we have been discussing at this conference.

Disclosure has become a ubiquitous policy response for a variety of problems. It is a very old remedy in the area of investments, but in the last 20 years, it has become a remedy for almost everything. In the United States, for example, virtually every state has passed a law requiring companies that have had a data breach to provide that information to whoever might have had their information compromised. Unfortunately, this is also an example of one of many totally ineffective applications of disclosure to address a real public policy problem. In general, I view myself as neutral on the question of disclosure. I think disclosure can work, but our research indicates that more often than not it does not.

▧ *A disclosure policy that works.* Let me start, then, with a disclosure law that has worked very successfully. Anyone who has eaten in a restaurant in Los Angeles has encountered one of the most effective disclosure laws that we have studied in this country—the Los Angeles County Restaurant Hygiene System. It is a simple system based on the county's detailed public health hygiene inspections. It was developed in response to one of those "gotcha" hidden-camera exposés that ABC News did in 1998. The county government imposed a requirement that all restaurants in the county display in their front window a grade of A, B, or C, based on the results of their most recent health inspection.

This very simple device of providing customers with information about the restaurant's last grade in the form of an A, B, or C turns out to be incredibly salient and has had a significant impact not only on the behavior of consumers but also on the behavior of restaurants, because restaurant owners could quickly see the revenue impact of having a change in their grade. Furthermore, a study by Ginger Jin and Phil Leslie confirmed that the system had a very positive impact on public health in the area, specifically in the reduction of restaurant-related, food-borne illness hospitalizations.[2]

■ *A failed disclosure policy.* Now contrast that with probably the least effective disclosure system we have studied—the Homeland Security Advisory System—which the Obama Administration has replaced. Even Tom Ridge, who built the system, acknowledged within a year and a half of its creation that it was ineffective, having virtually no effect on public safety.

Elements of a Successful Disclosure System. The key to success is understanding that effective disclosure systems do not operate in a vacuum; rather, they act on a set of human behaviors that already exist. Such systems are premised on how users already use information in a given set of transactions, so the disclosures are designed to respond to such behaviors.

Therefore, having a targeted transparency policy helps ensure that the information disclosed is salient to user decision making (**Figure 1**). The information affects customers' perceptions, leading to changes in customers' behaviors. Such changes, in turn, affect the discloser's perception and behavior. Action is induced by information and thus leads to a full cycle of behavioral change. A targeted transparency system, in its best case, requires additional information to correct for information asymmetry problems on the part of the discloser. This process engenders changes in behavior and improvements in the system.

Thus, it is clear why Los Angeles County's system works so well and why the Homeland Security Advisory System quickly became fodder for David Letterman and Jay Leno. Los Angeles County's system is deeply embedded in user behavior. Users get the information they need at the right time and in the right place. The Homeland Security Advisory System offered no actionable information. Beyond being vigilant, users had no idea what they were supposed to do. Therefore, perceptions and behaviors did not change.

Another example standing in stark contrast to Los Angeles County's system is the restaurant hygiene system used in San Francisco. A system similar to Los Angeles County's was originally proposed for San Francisco, but the

---

[2]Ginger Zhe Jin and Phillip Leslie, "The Effects of Information on Product Quality: Evidence from Restaurant Hygiene Grade Cards," *Quarterly Journal of Economics*, vol. 118, no. 2 (May 2003):409–451.

Figure 1.   Transparency Effectiveness: Action Cycle

With Transparency Policy

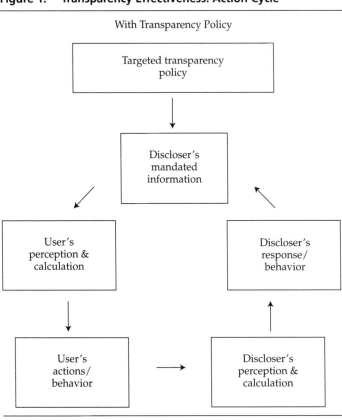

restaurant industry resisted the proposal, and the city finally passed a weak-
ened version in which information on hygiene is available in the back of the
restaurant and presented in the form of a detailed health inspection report. The
system has had no impact, which is not surprising because it is not embedded
in the way users or restaurant owners make decisions.

Therefore, any disclosure system in the financial area has to be embedded
in the way investors are making their decisions and, subsequently, what that
means for the disclosing side. Furthermore, information asymmetry must be
present. Otherwise, there is no need for disclosure. Next, users must have both
the will and the capacity to improve their choices, and disclosers must have
the capacity to improve their performance.

Disclosure System Architecture. A second set of related issues is what I call the architecture of a system—that is, how we actually devise information. The Los Angeles County system is a great example because it gathers disaggregated information and aggregates it into a single grade. A few things need to be in place to do this:

- Consensus metrics. All parties need to agree on valid measures of the behavior they are trying to effect.

- Intermediaries. Third parties who can help parse information are essential to the process.

- Acceptability of variable results. All parties need to agree whether it is acceptable that some people act on information in one way and others in a different way.

Once all these conditions are present, we can start conceptualizing the structure of the information and thus design the architecture of the transparency system to make it most effective.

An example of an incredibly disaggregated transparency system is that used for financial disclosure, which is premised, in theory, on very strong third-party intermediaries with the skills and incentives to both parse data and act as agents for their principals; however, they often do not.

Other federal laws have similar structures that retard them from working well. For example, a federally required drinking water contaminant report consisting of incredibly disaggregated data is issued every year. Most users find it impenetrable, which ultimately means they cannot act upon it.

Somewhat more helpful is the nutritional labeling system, which presents customers with a degree of detailed data but also attempts to aggregate that data by using expert judgment in the form of a recommended daily allowance.

One of the most interesting and effective systems in recent times was the highway rollover standard that was established because of the SUV rollover problems that occurred in 2000. The system aggregated an array of data through the use of expert judgment to create a five-star rating system for SUVs. It had an enormous impact on the fleet of cars the auto industry was offering.

Stirring the Debate. With these precepts in mind, consider some ideas for a financial disclosure system aimed at the home mortgage market, which I offer less as a finished solution than as a way to stir the debate. Consider something similar to the rollover standards for SUVs to give people a sense of the likelihood that their mortgages will "tip over." It could be a multistar rating presented to customers at a time when they can act on the information. It might include characteristics related to their credit history, their human capital, and the current housing market balanced against the type of mortgage they are considering. The result could be a rating for each potential mortgage product, thus giving customers a metric to act upon.

Ultimately, all discussions must come back to these points: understanding what users need, how they act, and how to fashion policies that the public finds actionable.

Henriette Prast

Assume that you decide to live up to your New Year's resolution. You decide to start saving and pay off your debt, and because you know you have self-control problems, you also decide to close your line of credit. You go to your bank's website, and with a few mouse clicks you are able to open a savings account. But when you try to close your credit line, you find, after much searching, the following instructions:

> If you want to close a credit line, please visit your local branch or call during regular office hours and ask for the appropriate form. When sending in the completed form make sure to include a copy of your passport and that of your ex-partner.

Banks want customers to open additional accounts, so they make the process simple. They do not want customers to close credit lines, so they make the process difficult and burdensome. They understand that if they create enough subtle barriers, customers may reconsider and change their minds or simply give up. This tactic is part of a business model that exploits financial consumers' irrationalities. It is part of what is being described as a behavioral industrial organization, which is what I want to discuss today.

Consumer Financial Protection and the Netherlands. First, however, consider the Netherlands. It has a social security program that is not connected to individuals' labor histories. Everyone who has lived long enough in the Netherlands and has turned 65 will receive an annuity of about $1,000 each month. It is pay-as-you-go, so a lot of taxpayers' money goes into it because contributions are not sufficient. Furthermore, saving for retirement is mandatory for almost all employees, but they do not need to save for tuition or healthcare because the government provides these items.

Yet, consumer financial protection is an issue in the Netherlands because a growing number of the self-employed do not save for retirement. Such saving is not mandatory for the self-employed, so they do not do it. In addition, employees are facing several challenges. First, they are dealing with a risk shift—more risk with lower replacement ratios. Second, plans are afoot to raise the eligibility age for social security and retirement. Furthermore, because of the financial crisis, consumers have a low level of trust in the financial sector.

Banks have failed, investors have lost money, and the taxpayers have had to rescue the banks. Finally, there is a concern that people are taking on mortgages that they cannot afford. The IMF, in fact, has named this as a source of instability in its financial analysis of the Netherlands.

Behavioral Industrial Organization. A sad fact of modern life is that banking technology has made it harder for people to exert self-control and use commitment mechanisms. In the 1950s, we saved money in a piggy bank and paid cash for almost everything. The use of money was tangible and thus reminded us of its real impact on our personal finances. Today, I can go to a website for designer clothing and spend money seven days a week, 24 hours a day. The website will even remember my credit card number. In the not too distant future, we will be able to pay by running our fingerprints over a scanner. The first experiments are already under way in certain supermarkets in the Netherlands. Money slips away quickly and easily, and soon we will not be able to leave it at home.

Behavioral industrial organization is a means by which businesses can exploit the irrationalities of their consumers. People, in fact, can be distracted rather than helped by more information.

■ *Too much information.* A recent study indicates that disclosure may crowd out the intrinsic motivation of financial advisers to be honest.[3] The study examines two groups of advisers on mortgages—one group has to disclose its fee; the other group does not. The study found that the advisers who had to disclose their fees more aggressively tended to recommend mortgages that paid them the highest fee, and customers were more likely to buy such mortgages. The reasoning follows along these lines: The advisers know that their customers can see how much money they will earn, yet they assume that the customers will discount that in their decision making, which the customers do because they assume the recommended product must be the best because of its price. Otherwise, the advisers would be ashamed to recommend it.

Consider another behaviorally informed evaluation of traditional policy. Some people have difficulty saving but would pay off a mortgage before they eat. In their case, buying an expensive home with a high mortgage can become a self-control mechanism. In fact, Laibson, Repetto, and Tobacman show that hyperbolic households hold more illiquid wealth, which cannot be dissaved

---

[3]Daylian M. Cain, George Loewenstein, and Don A. Moore, "When Sunlight Fails to Disinfect: Understanding the Perverse Effects of Disclosing Conflicts of Interest," *Journal of Consumer Research*, vol. 37, no. 5 (February 2011):836–857.

and which elevates wealth at retirement.[4] But if these households are not allowed to buy an expensive home and take out a high mortgage that they will pay off at high speed, then the mechanism is not allowed to materialize.

Now consider some traditional and alternative techniques to help people with health-related behavior. Some states require chain restaurants to post calorie information next to the price. Unfortunately, experiments show that not only does this disclosure system not work; it leads to more calorie consumption by those people who are on a diet because they think, "Oh, it is just 65 calories. I can take another one." This behavioral outcome is similar to results found on research on nutrition labels. A product may have zero fat but may be loaded with sugar to compensate for the loss of the fat. People see zero fat on the label and end up eating so much that they consume more calories than they might have otherwise.[5]

■ *A strategy that works.* What *does* work is evidenced by an interesting experiment—namely, cash for cookies. In university restaurants, students are allowed to pay with their debit cards, but in certain restaurants during the experiment, students had to pay for snacks, soft drinks, and sweet desserts with cash. In those restaurants where the cash-for-cookie system was introduced, students consumed more vegetables, more fruits, more water, more milk, and fewer snacks, soft drinks, and cookies. The small effort of having to take out cash encourages people to leave cash at home if they are planning to eat healthy.

Consumer Bank Reform in the Netherlands. In response to the financial crisis, banks in the Netherlands have drawn up a code that they must comply with by law or explain why they do not. In the code, financial consumers are center stage. For example, in the product approval process, it should be explained how the interests of investors have been taken into account, how bonuses are limited, and how other management decisions have been made. Top management must adopt an ethical statement, and permanent education is required for executive and nonexecutive board members.

I was on the monitoring committee for this code to judge whether banks comply or explain their behavior adequately. We had to report to the finance minister and the banking association. We concluded that the banks still have a long way to go—to put it very generously—and that banks need guidance on how to

---

[4]D. Laibson, A. Repetto, and J. Tobacman, "A Debt Puzzle," in *Knowledge, Information and Expectations in Modern Economics: In Honor of Edmund S. Phelps*, edited by P. Aghion, R. Frydman, J. Stiglitz, and M. Woodford (Princeton, NJ: Princeton University Press, 2003):228–266.

[5]Henriëtte Prast, "A Behavioral Economics Approach to Public Health: Theory and Policy Implications," *European Journal of Consumer Law*, vol. 4 (2011):723–747.

put financial customers first. I have several suggestions based on the introduction of mechanisms that use consumer biases in the interest of consumers:

1. Eliminate tactics that exploit consumer biases in the banks' favor, such as making it difficult to close a credit line. The number of mouse clicks needed to close a credit line should not exceed the number of mouse clicks needed to take out a loan or open an account.

2. Stop teasing people with high rates of interest in order to induce them to open savings accounts, only to let those interest rates fall unless the contract is changed. Some customers make the effort to maintain the high rate, but many do not.

3. Stop paying salaries by the month. Biweekly wage payments help people manage their finances and can be enabled with inexpensive changes to payment technology.

4. Try to develop a cash-for-cookies equivalent to discourage people from paying high interest rates on loans they may not need.

Conclusion. Traditional policy, which assumes that people are rational, may be ineffective or even counterproductive. Libertarian paternalism helps people who need help without limiting the freedom of choice of those who do not need help.

RESEARCH FOUNDATION
CONTRIBUTION FORM

☑ **Yes**, I want the Research Foundation to continue to fund innovative research that advances the investment management profession. Please accept my tax-deductible contribution at the following level:

Thought Leadership Circle ....US$1,000,000 or more
Named Endowment ....US$100,000 to US$999,999
Research Fellow............................ US$10,000 to US$99,999
Contributing Donor........................ US$1,000 to US$9,999
Friend .... Up to US$999

I would like to donate $ _____.

☐ My check is enclosed (payable to the Research Foundation of CFA Institute).
☐ I would like to donate appreciated securities (send me information).
☐ Please charge my donation to my credit card.

■ VISA ■ MC ■ Amex ■ Diners ■ Corporate ■ Personal

Card Number

____/____

Expiration Date   Name on card   P L E A S E   P R I N T

☐ Corporate Card
☐ Personal Card

Signature

☐ This is a pledge. Please bill me for my donation of $ _____
☐ I would like recognition of my donation to be:

■ Individual donation   ■ Corporate donation   ■ Different individual

PLEASE PRINT NAME OR COMPANY NAME AS YOU WOULD LIKE IT TO APPEAR

PLEASE PRINT   ☐ Mr. ☐ Mrs. ☐ Ms.   MEMBER NUMBER_____

Last Name (Family Name)   First   Middle Initial

Title

Address

City   State/Province   Countr y ZIP/Postal Code

Please mail this completed form with your contribution to:
The Research Foundation of CFA Institute • P.O. Box 2082
Charlottesville, VA 22902-2082 USA

For more on the Research Foundation of CFA Institute, please visit www.cfainstitute.org/about/foundation/.